YOU CAN

U

with
beakman & jax

way More
Science Stuff You Can Do

by JOK CHURCH

Andrews and McMeel
A Universal Press Syndicate Company
Kansas City

Library of Congress Cataloging-in-Publication Data

Church, Jok.
      You can with Beakman & Jax : way more science
stuff you can do / by Jok Church.
                p.   cm.
      ISBN: 0-8362-7043-6 : $8.95
      1. Science Experiments—Juvenile literature. 2. Science-
-Miscellanea—Juvenile literature. 3. Science—Comic books,
strips, etc. Juvenile literature. [1. Science—Experiments.
2. Experiments. 3. Science—Miscellanea.] I. Title. II. Title:
You can with Beakman & Jax.

                                        CIP
                                        AC

NOTE TO PARENTS:

You Can with Beakman & Jax: Way More Science Stuff You Can *Do* is intended to be educational and informative. It contains relatively simple science experiments designed to interest children. Many of the experiments require adult supervision. We strongly recommend that before you allow children to conduct any of the experiments in this book that you read the experiment in its entirety and make your own determination as to the safest way of conducting the experiment.

CONTENTS

Stuff *You Can* Do to Figure Out . . .

Greetings:

This book thanks my friends for their help in turning a comic strip into a book. They are completely different things and care must taken to create one from the other. Andrews and McMeel editor Dorothy O'Brien and graphics wizards Julie Phillips and Susan Patton have my thanks.

Before any of the experiments go into the funnies, they go into and consume the home of Adam Ciesielski and he has my thanks for his support.

The love of understanding was grown in me by my ninth-grade science teacher Richard Etling. My English teacher Willie Poston taught me how to say so out loud.

The first person who told me to go write something was Ingrid Swanberg-Markhardt. I love her for that and lots more reasons.

Thanks to those of you who write me the questions. Thanks for teaching me all the things that I know.

Lisa Tarry is my editor at Universal Press Syndicate and she and I together massage these questions into answers we all can understand.

Before she sees them, the answers often get tried out on Glenn Corey who makes me feel really lucky.

My friends John Breuer, Paul Schwartz and Zack Weingart help me understand much about me and they have my thanks and love.

Thanks also to Mary Urban, Jean Spreen, Laura Jordan, Barb Thompson, Bev Shiels, Rita Denton, Joyce Mott, Elena Fallon, Alan McDermott, Lee Salem, Kathy Andrews and John and Susan McMeel.

A good question is a very powerful thing.
Keep answering them.

—Jok

*For the staff and volunteers of
the San Rafael Public Library*

and for library workers everywhere.

Dear Reader:

⚠ Please look for this special caution sign throughout this book. When you see this sign, it means that you need to ask a grown-up for help.

This is a book for families to use together so the grown-ups in your family should be happy to work with you.

Show your family this page.

Remember, look for this sign. It is very important. ⚠

Beakman

Beakman

Jax Place

Jax Place

Dear Jax,

If you have acid in your stomach, why don't you melt?

Jason Valenta Northhampton, Massachusetts

Dear Jason,

Your stomach does have acid inside of it – hydrochloric acid – strong enough to eat through a piece of the metal zinc.

The reason your stomach isn't destroyed by the acid is our old friend snot, which is also called mucus.

Mucus is thick, sticky, slimy and gooey. And it's a good thing. The inside of your stomach is covered with it. That layer of snot protects the stomach from its own acid. In fact, the miracle of mucus protects many parts of our bodies – some parts that even I will not mention here.

Jax Place

EXPERIMENT #1

Make Some Fake Snot

WHAT YOU NEED: Light corn syrup - unflavored gelatin - measuring cup - water - family permission - microwave oven or stove

WHAT TO DO: Heat ½ cup water just until it boils. Remove heat. Sprinkle in 3 envelopes of unflavored gelatin. Let it soften a few minutes and stir with a fork. Add enough corn syrup to make 1 cup of thick glop. Stir with the fork and lift out the long strands of gunk.

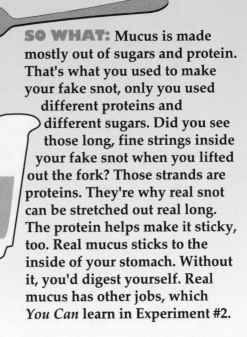

SO WHAT: Mucus is made mostly out of sugars and protein. That's what you used to make your fake snot, only you used different proteins and different sugars. Did you see those long, fine strings inside your fake snot when you lifted out the fork? Those strands are proteins. They're why real snot can be stretched out real long. The protein helps make it sticky, too. Real mucus sticks to the inside of your stomach. Without it, you'd digest yourself. Real mucus has other jobs, which *You Can* learn in Experiment #2.

Now Make Some Fake Boogers

EXPERIMENT #2

WHAT YOU NEED: Your fake snot from Experiment #1 - vacuum cleaner

WHAT TO DO: Ask someone who knows to show you the right way to change the vacuum cleaner bag. (*You Can* sell everyone on the idea of doing this experiment because you'll now *be able to help out around the house*.) Go outside with the dirt bag and your fake snot. Blow a bit of the dust from the vacuum cleaner. It's very fine and is a bad thing to breathe into our bodies. Dump a pinch of the finest dust onto your fake snot. Now stir it up. Look closely into the goo from the side. You just made fake boogers!

SO WHAT: The fine dust got trapped and suspended in the thick fake snot. That's the idea of having mucus in your nose. We use it to trap all the dust, pollen and junk that's floating in the air. Sometimes when you blow your nose, out comes gross black stuff. It's usually mucus with trapped dust. It's healthier to keep that kind of dirt outside of our bodies. And with the miracle of snot on guard, most of the schmutz is trapped and then blown out in boogers.

P.S. from Beakman: Be sure to keep this recipe in mind for Halloween. *You Can* never have too much thick, gooey, sticky, slimy stuff at Halloween.

9

Dear Jax,

Why do you hear the ocean in seashells?

Lisa Ricke
Savage,
Minnesota

Dear Jax,

Is it true that in the Southern Hemisphere water swirls down the drain the opposite way it swirls in the Northern Hemisphere?

Alisha Greten
Nashville, Illinois

Dear Lisa and Alisha,

I'm answering your questions together because in a strange way they are connected to each other.

Both questions have to do with what's already there. Stuff that's just there in the background and a part of our environment we call ambient (AM-bee-ent). Sink drains and seashells both concentrate things that are ambient.

Seashells concentrate ambient sound. Sink and tub drains concentrate ambient motion in the water.

Jax Place
Jax Place

Hearing Things

WHAT YOU NEED: paper towel tube
Optional: roll of foil or plastic wrap

WHAT TO DO: Hold the tube (or roll of foil) up to your ear. Use your hand to close the other end. Be very quiet. Move the roll in and out from your ear. Try opening and closing the other end by moving your fingers. Listen for the changes that happen when you move your fingers to open and close the tube.

WHAT IS GOING ON: Even though it's not as pretty, your tube works just like a seashell. Both are sound chambers. Both pick up and bounce ambient sound waves – the sounds that are already there. All these sounds bouncing around inside the tube (or the seashell) is what you hear. It's not really the ocean.

P.S. from Beakman: The cardboard tube will sound like the ocean just about anywhere. That's because even the quietest of places still has some sound in it. Like the sounds coming from you!

Reversing the Spin You're In

WHAT YOU NEED: A sink full of water - your finger - an open mind

WHAT TO DO: When you see a whirlpool in a draining sink, stick your finger in the whirlpool and draw circles in the water in the opposite direction of the swirl. Do it quickly and the whirlpool just reverses and spins the other way!

SO WHAT: People hate hearing this, but the hemisphere you're in has nothing to do with the way water swirls down a sink drain. In really big bodies of water – like oceans – the spin of the Earth does affect currents. It's called the Coriolis force. But sinks, tubs and even lakes are too small to be affected by it.

WHAT IS GOING ON: As the water falls into the drain, the ambient motion of the water has to go somewhere; it can't just disappear. It forces the water into a quick spin. The direction of the spin has to do with the direction of the motion already in the water – not with the rotation of the planet.

12

Dear Beakman,

How do the bar codes at the grocery store work?

Justin Child
Placerville,
California

Dear Justin,

If you're a cash register, the center of the universe is Dayton, Ohio – the home of a cloister called the Uniform Code Council.

Like a group of dutiful business monks, the people at the UCC are dedicated to spreading their vision of the Universal Product Code. (Anything being *universal* is a very heavy concept. Look it up.)

The UCC's UPC bar codes are read by laser beams. But *humans* with lots of patience *can* translate them, too. Keep in mind that machines can do this entire experiment in less than 1 second.

Beakman

Beakman Place

EXPERIMENT #1

Decode the Bar Code

WHAT YOU NEED: Paper and pencil - this book - patience

WHAT TO DO: There are 12 digits in a UPC. Each digit is separated into 7 tiny slices. Read the 12 digits by reading the slices. If a slice is black, write down a 1. If it's white, write down a 0. Do this for all 12. To get the UPC, match your list of 1's and 0's to the Code Key. See if you get the 12 correct UPC digits by reading the upside-down line in a mirror.

Code Key

Digit Value	Left Binary Code	Right Binary Code
0	0001101	1110010
1	0011001	1100110
2	0010011	1101100
3	0111101	1000010
4	0100011	1011100
5	0110001	1001110
6	0101111	1010000
7	0111011	1000100
8	0110111	1001000
9	0001011	1110100

On the left-hand side of the center code, use the left codes. Switch to the right codes on the right side of the center code. This mirror image coding lets the scanner read the numbers in either direction.

medium-sized can of Hershey's chocolate syrup.
number is for the Hershey's company. The product code is for a
The UPC number is 0-34000-31500-0. The manufacturer's code

P.S. from Jax:

Know the Code

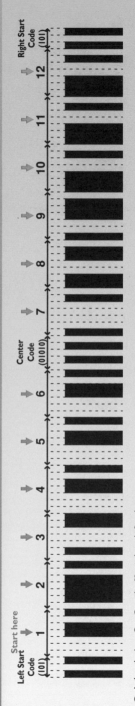

The UCC proclaims these to be: "human readable numbers."

The first 6 digits are a particular manufacturer's code. Every product they make will begin with these same 6 digits. This number is handed down by the UCC.

The 5 digit item number is given to the product by the company that makes it. That gives them 99,999 things they can make.

This is a *check digit*. It's the answer to a math problem designed to be sure the scanner read the right code number.

Amaze your friends! Fool the teacher! *You Can* always guess the last number of a UPC code. Use the "human readable numbers" from any 12-digit UPC code: Add the sum of the odd-spaced digits (the 1st, 3rd, 5th, 7th, 9th). Multiply the sum by 3. Save that as answer #1. Add up the even-spaced digits of the code (Don't include the check digit! That's the one you're guessing). Add that answer to answer #1. The check digit will be whatever number you have to add to your last answer to get it up to the next multiple of 10.

Dear Jax,

Why does my hair get curly when the humidity goes up?

Lisa Lee
Kansas City,
Missouri

Dear Lisa,

Sounds like you've had a problem getting your *do* just right. Humidity is dampness in the air, and it's one of the reasons why you hear so much about people having good-hair days and bad-hair days. Humidity (hu-MID-it-tee) makes hair big.

People say *big hair* a lot. Big hair usually means that someone's hairdo is big and puffy like Dolly Parton or Tina Turner. But the big hair I'm talking about is when places in your hairs actually get bigger and fatter. Humidity changes their shape and can frizz out your coiffure.

Jax Place
Jax Place

Huge Hairs

WHAT YOU NEED: A paper-wrapped soda straw

WHAT TO DO: Talk your family into a trip to the burger place. Explain that it's for the advancement of scientific knowledge. They'll like that. Grab a straw. Stand the straw up on the table and push the paper wrapper down around the straw until it's as short as it can be (Figure 1). Lay the compressed wrapper on the table. Use your straw to put just 1 drop of soda pop (or water) on the wrapper. Besides getting a burger out of the deal, what happens?

Fig. I

WHAT IS GOING ON: The tight folds of paper absorb the water and get fatter. That makes the wrapper twist and bend. Every time you put another drop on the wrapper (Figure 2), it twists and bends until it can't hold any more water. Your hair absorbs water from damp air. It twists and bends, too. This is not really getting curly. It's getting frizzy.

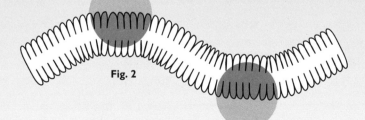

Fig. 2

17

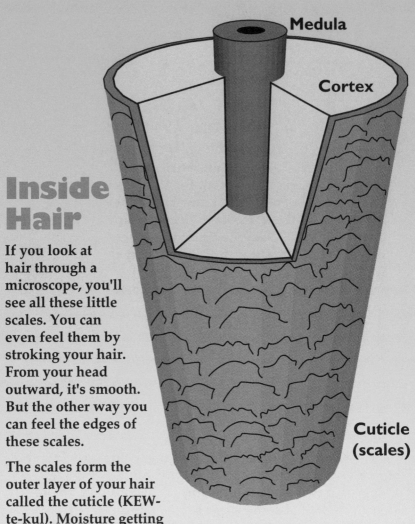

Medula

Cortex

Cuticle (scales)

Inside Hair

If you look at hair through a microscope, you'll see all these little scales. You can even feel them by stroking your hair. From your head outward, it's smooth. But the other way you can feel the edges of these scales.

The scales form the outer layer of your hair called the cuticle (KEW-te-kul). Moisture getting into the cuticle is a lot like your experiment.

In other hair happenings: Your hair color is in the cortex of the hair.

I hate the idea of people being average. But the average person has 100,000 hairs on her or his head.

You lose between 50 and 100 hairs every day!

Dear Beakman,

How does a blimp work?

Leslie Swales
Stow, Ohio

Dear Leslie,

You probably see lots of blimps there in Stow because it's so close to Akron, Ohio – where blimps come from.

To fly, a blimp doesn't have to do much work at all. The air that's pushing against us all the time pushes a blimp up into the sky. So the air does the real work of pushing up the blimp.

Blimps float in the air because they weigh less than the air.

It's very much like a cork floating in water.

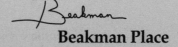

Beakman Place

19

A Thinking Game

WHAT YOU NEED: An active imagination

WHAT TO DO: Pretend this drawing is an elevator or a lift. There are 7 people inside. If we took out 3, what would change? Think about it for a minute. What would be the same? What would be different?

Mirror Message:

WHAT'S THE SAME: The elevator is the same size. It takes up the same amount of space.

WHAT'S DIFFERENT: The elevator weighs less.

SO WHAT: When something takes up the same amount of space but weighs less, we say that it has lower density (DEN-sa-tee). Stuff that's high-density pushes low-density stuff up.

P.S. from Jax: Hot air is less dense than cold air. The bag flew because the cold air pushed it up, just like a cork is pushed up in a glass of water. And just like a blimp is pushed up into the sky.

Blimps are not filled with hot air. They're filled with the gas helium. Both hot-air balloons and blimps are pushed up in the sky because they are filled with gases that have a lower density than the air.

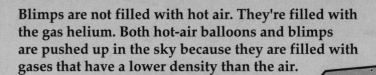

Make a Lighter-Than-Air Ship

WHAT YOU NEED: Plastic bag - hair dryer - permission to use the hair dryer or a grown-up helper - tape

WHAT TO DO: Put the bag over the dryer's nozzle. Put one piece of tape around the nozzle like in the drawing. Do NOT tape the bag to the dryer. The bag should slide up or down on the nozzle. Take the bag off the dryer. Turn on the dryer to warm it up. Put the bag over the nozzle and turn the dryer on high. In a few seconds, let go of the bag.

Dear Jax,

Why do bubbles pop?

Kyle Oholendt
San Antonio,
Texas

Dear Kyle,

Bubbles pop for 1 reason. They get holes. Holes happen when something dry touches the bubble.

It can be your finger or even a piece of dust. Dry stuff touching bubbles pops them.

If you could blow a bubble in a dust-free room, it would not pop. It would just slowly lose its air like a balloon loses its air.

My friend Louie Pearl makes bubble toys. He blew a bubble that lasted for 30 days! It was blown in a jar.

You Can make great bubble stuff to see how bubbles pop!

Jax Place
Jax Place

Tremendous Bubbles Formula

Better and Lots Cheaper

WHAT YOU NEED: Liquid dishwashing soap - glycerine (from drugstore) - gallon jug

WHAT TO DO: Add $2/3$ cup of the soap to a gallon of water. Add the soap last so you don't get a jug full of suds. Add 1 tablespoon of glycerine, which will help your bubbles last longer. Ask the people at the drugstore for it. You may want to experiment by trying things like Jell-O, Certo or even sugar instead. I use glycerine. Use this for your experiment and just for fun.

IMPORTANT: The dish soap you use has to be clear or transparent. Do *not* use any lotion-type soaps. Also, the more expensive brands work better for bubbles. I use Dawn or Ajax, but *You Can* try others. Soap for a dishwashing machine will not work.

Construct a Mega-Bubble

WHAT YOU NEED: Flashlight - soda straw - plastic coffee can lid - bubble formula - dark room

WHAT TO DO: Set up the lid and flashlight like in the drawing. Dump a spoonful of your bubble formula into the lid. Wet the lid and the straw with the bubble stuff. Get it really wet. Turn off the lights. Turn on the flashlight. Use the straw to blow a bubble on the lid. Pull the straw out of the bubble. Sit and watch the bubble. It will get thin on top and thick on the bottom. You'll be able to see thin spots form. You'll also see *lots* of colors.

Look closely at the thin spots. You'll be able to see little dots. That's dust hitting and popping the bubble.

Try this: Wet your finger really well in the bubble formula. Stick it into the bubble. It won't break!

P.S. from Beakman: Grown-ups in their 40s or 50s will love this experiment. The wild and crazy colors in the bubbles will remind them of the olden times in the 1960s.

Dear Jax,

Why do you burp?

Joshua Hardin
Fremont,
California

Dear Joshua,

Ah yes, burping! An excellent way to achieve balance!

You say *burp*. I say *belch*. Neither name sounds very polite, even though the idea here is to learn why.

Burp/belch: *vb* 1: to expel gas suddenly from the stomach through the mouth; 2: to erupt or explode. Remind you of any particular person in your family?

The truth is we all burp. We do it because the pressure of gases in our stomachs is higher than the air pressure outside. So a burp balances them. That's right – burps are about balance. Pretty cosmic, huh?

Jax Place
Jax Place

On-Demand Burping

WHAT YOU NEED: Just your sweet self

WHAT TO DO: Try to forget that you are not eating anything right now. Take a swallow of air. Pretend the air is a big sandwich. Don't breathe it. Swallow it. You might want to take a couple swallows of air. Now relax. Let your shoulders fall. Feel the muscles in your face go limp. You'll burp!

SO WHAT: You just learned something that we all pretty much forget while we're eating – that we swallow air along with food.

Sometimes a meal is so good, we gorge ourselves. You know, a pig-out. People usually burp after a meal like that because they've pushed lots of air into their stomachs.

In some parts of the world, a burp is a way of offering a compliment to the host for a fine meal. Now that you can burp when you want, you'd fit right in.

Mirror Message:

Okay, so now you're going to run around burping all the time. Believe me, you'll get over it. In the meantime, teach your friends. Then You Can gross out each other and leave everyone else alone.

P.S. from Beakman: The symbol behind the words on this page has nothing whatever to do with pizza-eating turtles. Also, it does NOT mean karate. It's a yin-yang, and it's the symbol for balance.

26

Like a Balloon

This is a simple drawing of our insides. You might say these are our guts. Gases build up pressure in 2 different ways. The first way is that while we're swallowing food, we're also swallowing air along with it.

The air inflates our stomach like a balloon. That means the air inside the stomach is pushing harder than the air outside the stomach.

Mouth

The next thing that makes gas is all the chemicals in our stomachs. We make acids there to start breaking down food. Pour some vinegar on a bit of baking soda. It will make gas a lot like our stomachs do. That gas is a burp, too. Gases building up in our stomachs have to get out to maintain balance. And there are just 2 places they can go. Think hard. You'll figure out for yourself the other place they can go.

A burp feels good. Your stomach gets all inflated. A burp lets the pressure out and that just feels better.

Stomach

Small Intestine

Large Intestine

Appendix

You burp about 15 times a day.

Rectum

Dear Beakman,

How does cement get hard?

Paul Davison
Brooklyn Park,
Minnesota

Dear Paul,

Cement is not something that gets wet, then just dries out and gets all hard. Cement does not dry. It can even get hard under water – like when we use cement to make concrete bridges.

Cement and other similar compounds undergo chemical reactions when we add water. New chemicals are made that bind to each other and get hard. This is not drying. We call it *curing*.

Beakman
Beakman Place

EXPERIMENT #1

Try It with Some Plaster

WHAT YOU NEED: Plaster of Paris (from a hardware store) - water - old bowl - family permission and help

WHAT TO DO: Read the directions and mix up 1 cup of plaster. Keep stirring till it gets really thick – about 5 minutes. Smoosh the plaster into the bottom of the bowl. Gently trickle in 2 or 3 cups water. Let the water float on top of the plaster. Ignore the whole thing for an hour. Now pour off the water. What's inside?

WHAT TO DO: Plaster and cement cure in similar ways. New chemicals are formed when water is added. You sped up the chemical reaction when you overmixed it. The plaster should have gotten warm. Heat is another product of the chemical reaction that's going on.

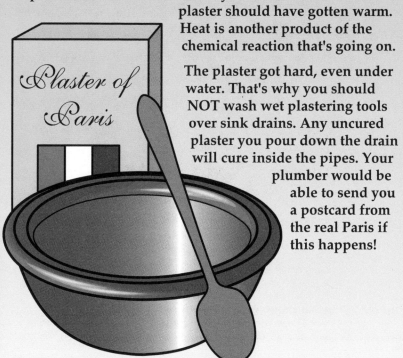

The plaster got hard, even under water. That's why you should NOT wash wet plastering tools over sink drains. Any uncured plaster you pour down the drain will cure inside the pipes. Your plumber would be able to send you a postcard from the real Paris if this happens!

EXPERIMENT #2

String Up a Balloon

WHAT YOU NEED: Mix up some plaster. Soak some string in uncured plaster and wrap the string around the balloon. Keep wrapping until the balloon is nearly covered with plastered string. When the plaster cures, pop the balloon.

WHAT TO DO:

Okay, you're right. This is not really an experiment. It's a crafts project. (There's nothing like a cement question to get me in the holiday mood.) You just made a holiday ornament that looks like a ball made out of lace. Make several. Hang them up on whatever your particular holiday calls for hanging things on.

P.S. from Jax: Concrete is made out of cement mixed with sand, gravel and water. To make brick mortar, we leave out the gravel. In the 1700s, in North America, the colonists made cement out of ground-up oyster shells.

Dear Beakman,

How does milk turn into cheese?

Danielle Beck
San Francisco,
California

Dear Danielle,

The stuff that Little Miss Muffet was eating when the spider sat down beside her is the stuff that *You Can* make cheese out of: curds and whey.

Milk is not really just a liquid. Milk is made out of solid particles floating in liquid. Cheese is pretty much the solid particles from milk *without* the liquid.

You Can make a delicious cheese at home, and you don't have to know any spiders to do it.

Beakman
Beakman Place

Curdle Some Milk

WHAT YOU NEED: ½ cup homogenized milk - 2 tablespoons vinegar

WHAT TO DO: Put the first tablespoon of vinegar into the milk and stir it up. Use the spoon to ladle through the milk, lifting and pouring. Add the rest of the vinegar and keep ladling. Look carefully at the milk as it flows off the spoon. Vinegar is a kind of acid – acetic acid. What does it do to milk?

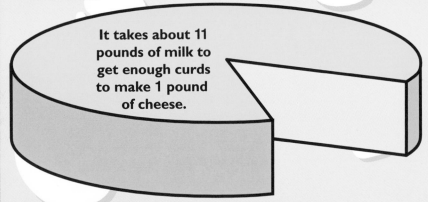

It takes about 11 pounds of milk to get enough curds to make 1 pound of cheese.

WHAT IS GOING ON: That was pretty awful, wasn't it? The milk got all lumpy and cruddy. Most important, it got thick, which is the first part of making cheese.

Added bacteria that eat the sugars in milk make another kind of acid as their waste – lactic acid — and it thickens milk.

Next, cheese-makers add rennet, which is a chemical discovered in the fourth stomach of cows. It separates milk into whey (WAY), the liquid; and curds, the solids.

EXPERIMENT #2

Make Some Cheese

WHAT YOU NEED: Carton of non-fat cottage cheese (*NOT* low-fat) – salt – a favorite herb, like thyme – old white T-shirt – plenty of patience – permission and help from your family

WHAT TO DO: Mix 1 teaspoon of salt into the cottage cheese. Add ½ teaspoon of your herb. Mix this up really well.

Cut up the old T-shirt so that you have one flat piece of cloth – like the front or back of the shirt. Rinse the shirt in clear plain water and wring it out. Do this a couple of times.

Lay the cloth out and plop the cottage cheese onto it. Lift up the cloth and twist it tightly into a ball.

SALT of the

NON-FAT Cottage Cheese

THYME

> Read more about cheese in the encyclopedia at your library.

Hang it in a cool place where a rank smell won't bother you – like a garage, or basement, or maybe a brother or sister's room. It's going to ooze and drip and smell for more than a week.

In 10 days, peel off the cloth and enjoy with crackers. You just made *farmer's cheese.*

P.S. from Jax: Non-fat cottage cheese is pretty much curds with most of the whey already drained. You just did the last part in cheese-making. You dried and aged the curds.

33

Dear Jax,

Why is the color black hot?

Melanie Stevenson
Dearborn, Michigan

Dear Melanie,

Back in olden times in the 1960s, earthtones were hot. Now the hot colors are black, green and purple. Black is hot because it can make you look artistic and all groovy, especially black turtlenecks.

But I think you might be asking about *another* kind of hot – the temperature kind of hot.

Black things get hotter in sunlight because all colors turn into heat. Black gets hotter because it absorbs the most colors.

Jax Place
Jax Place

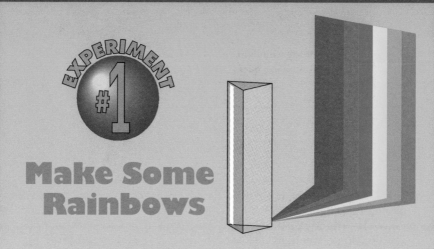

EXPERIMENT #1

Make Some Rainbows

WHAT YOU NEED: Prism – sunshine
Optional: shallow pan – mirror – water

WHAT TO DO: Use either of the drawings as a guide and make your own rainbow. If you use the water method, be sure to let the water get very still and to tilt the mirror slowly until you see colors.

WHAT IS GOING ON: What looks like white light is really all colors of light mixed together. We see colors because colored light bounces off things. *When we see something, we do not see the thing. We see light bouncing off the thing!*

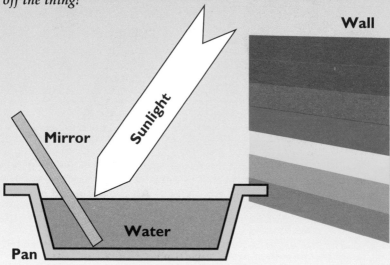

Wall

Mirror

Sunlight

Water

Pan

How Colors Bounce

Sunlight in **Reflected light bouncing back**

If something is yellow, it absorbs all colors of light except for yellow. It reflects, or bounces back, yellow light.

If something is blue, it absorbs all colors of light except for blue. It reflects, or bounces back, blue light.

Since all colors are reflected, no colors are absorbed and no heat is produced.

If something is red, it absorbs all colors of light except for red. It reflects, or bounces back, red light.

No colors are reflected. All colors are absorbed and converted into heat.

If something is white, it absorbs no colors of light. It reflects, or bounces back, all the colors of light.

If something is black, it absorbs all colors of light. It reflects, or bounces, no colors. All the absorbed colors turn into heat.

P.S. from Beakman: If no light is bouncing off something, then there isn't any color. That means there is no color at all in darkness.

Dear Beakman,

How do CD players work?

Tristan Nenna
South Bend,
Indiana

Dear Tristan,

The best way to understand how a CD player works is to make a *Mind Movie*. That's what I call making up a complicated vision with the power of your imagination.

To make a *Mind Movie*, get a friend or member of your family. Close your eyes and get all peaceful-like while your helper reads out loud from this book.

Imagine the things you're being told.

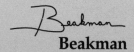
Beakman

CD Player:
The Mind Movie

Read this out loud in an even-toned voice. Don't rush this.
Give the listener lots of time to use her or his imagination.

Imagine you're in a long, long hallway. It's so long you can't
see the beginning in front of you or the end behind you. The
hallway is miles and miles long. You look up. Somehow,
someone has put bathtubs upside down on the ceiling. In
between the bathtubs are mirrors. As far as you can see up and
down the ceiling of the hallway are bathtubs and mirrors. For
miles of ceiling there are bathtubs and mirrors, upside
down on the ceiling. Then, everything gets dark!

You have a flashlight in one hand. You turn on the
light, point it up to the ceiling and start running.
Every time the light shines up and hits a
mirror, the light bounces right back down
at you. But when the light goes into a
tub, it scatters and gets lost and
you're left in the dark.

Now imagine that you can take notes while you're running. Every time the light bounces back down, you write a 1. When the light gets lost, you write a zero. After running for miles and miles, you'd have a whole sheet of paper filled with 1's and 0's. And those numbers are what a CD player uses to play back music and data. Now open your eyes and come back.

A real CD player doesn't use a flashlight. It uses a laser. And your weird ceiling is really a shiny disk covered with pits. If a CD didn't spin and were a hallway – like in your Mind Movie – it would be more than 4 miles long.

CDs play upside down, with the laser pointing up. The beginning of the disk is the center of the disk – the opposite of how a phonograph record works. (A phonograph record is what they used in olden times to listen to bands with names like *Strawberry Alarm Clock*.)

A CD player plays a sound that is based on numbers. It sees a new number 41,000 times a second!

P.S. from Jax: The width of a CD's track is so narrow you could lay 40 of them side by side under 1 human hair!

Dear Beakman,

How does a computer work?

Arthur Bond
Cockeysville,
Maryland

Dear Arthur,

Computers are very complicated things. How they work is really hard to explain in a page or two. But, I can give you a new way to think about computers. *You Can* think about them and they cannot think about you!

Computers are just machines that follow instructions we give them. We call the instructions a *program*. That means a computer is like a program-*player*. And the computer turns into anything – any kind of machine – we can tell it to.

With the right program, a computer can be a typewriter, a game, a musical instrument, or even a telescope. It can be any kind of machine we can program it to be. This is why the job of being a computer programmer is such a big deal.

Here's a secret: I don't use a pencil to draw this comic. I use a computer that has been turned into a drawing machine by the programs I play on it.

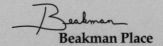
Beakman Place

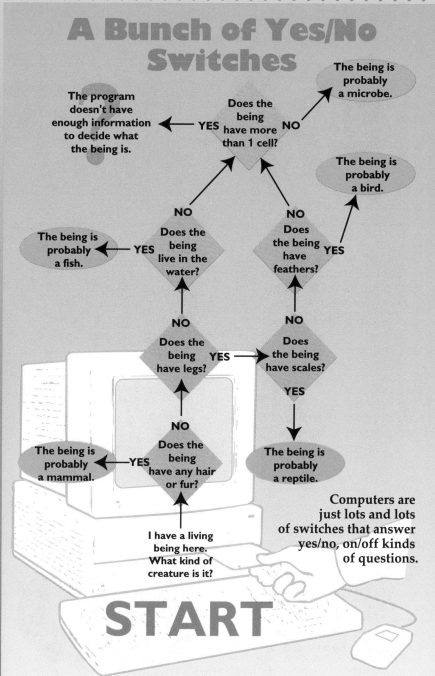

A Bunch of Yes/No Switches

The being is probably a microbe.

Does the being have more than 1 cell? — **YES** → The program doesn't have enough information to decide what the being is.

NO

NO → Does the being have more than 1 cell?

The being is probably a bird.

Does the being live in the water? — **YES** → The being is probably a fish.

NO

Does the being have feathers? — **YES** → (bird)

NO

Does the being have legs? — **YES** → Does the being have scales?

NO

NO

Does the being have scales? — **YES** → The being is probably a reptile.

Does the being have any hair or fur? — **YES** → The being is probably a mammal.

NO

I have a living being here. What kind of creature is it?

Computers are just lots and lots of switches that answer yes/no, on/off kinds of questions.

START

P.S. from Jax: When a mistake is written into a program, it's called a bug. The first bug was really a bug. A moth got caught in a switch in an early computer. Beakman's program has bugs, too. Try it with a moth or a snake as your being.

41

Computer Art

I want to draw a red blood cell. I start by drawing this shape on the computer. It's really a bunch of math that describes this curvy thing.

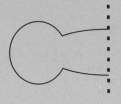

Next, I tell the computer program to spin the shape around the dotted line. I get this thing that looks like a bagel-shaped bird cage.

Now I tell the program to pretend the bird-cage-thing has a shiny surface and that there are 2 lights shining on it. What does it look like now?

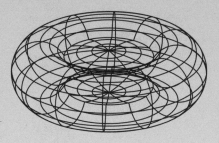

Lastly, each weird little area is given a color that represents how light or dark it would be if a light was shining on it. The areas together turn out to be a good drawing of a red blood cell!

Dear Beakman,

How does the quartz crystal in a watch work?

Billy Dellvow
Bath, Michigan

Dear Billy,

I love this question because *You Can* have such a great time getting the answer.

A quartz watch is the opposite of a Lifesaver™ sparking in your mouth! Isn't that cool?

You'll have to go into the closet for this — but just until you see the light.

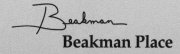
Beakman Place

Sparks in the Dark

WHAT YOU NEED: Mirror - roll of *Cryst-O-Mint* flavor Lifesaver™ candy - closet - towel

WHAT TO DO: Go into the closet and stuff the towel under the door so no light at all gets in. Look around for several minutes to adjust your eyes to the darkness. Pop one of the Lifesavers into your mouth. Look into the mirror and crunch down. You'll see your mouth light up with a white flash. Cool, huh?

P.S. from Jax: We know people all over the world read *You Can.* So, you might be in a country that doesn't sell Lifesavers™ candy. Try others. Look for a clear or white mint that is almost all sugar crystals. Experiment with several until you find one that works for you!

WHAT IS GOING ON: You just created *piezo electricity* (pee-AY-zo). Here's what it is: If you put *physical energy* into some crystals, they change it into electrical energy. The reverse is true, too. If you put *electrical energy into* these crystals, you get physical energy back out. That's how a quartz crystal watch works. A battery puts electrical energy into the quartz crystal, which vibrates at controlled speeds – such as 30,000 times a second. A computer chip then counts the vibrations to figure out the time. 30,000 vibrations equals 1 second.

Dear Jax,

How come when I look at something with 1 eye, things move back and forth when I open and close the other eye?

Shauna Bullee
Brandon, Manitoba

Dear Shauna,

Talk about your personal visions! You're able to make things move back and forth, just by blinking!? That sounds like an idea for a sitcom.

Anyway, back to reality. These things are not moving. You're noticing just 1 of the 2 views you have of the world that you usually see together.

We see 1 view with each of our eyes. Each view is different. But when the brain puts them together into 1 overall view, it could get really confusing unless 1 view kind of takes things over. We call that being dominant (DOM-in-ent).

Jax Place

Which Eye Rules?

WHAT YOU NEED: Your sweet self - this book

WHAT TO DO: Put this book 5 to 6 feet away from you. Make a ring with the fingers of your left hand. Reach out your arm to its full length. Look through the ring at the

You Can symbol on the next page with *both* of your eyes. You'll have to relax to get this to happen.

Slowly close, then open one eye at a time. The image will move for one eye and not move for the other eye. The eye that sees the unmoving image is your dominant eye.

SO WHAT: You're right- or left-handed, and the same sort of thing happens with your eyes. To help your brain put the eyes' different images together, 1 of those images is used as a kind of reference point. That's the dominant image.

find your dominant eye

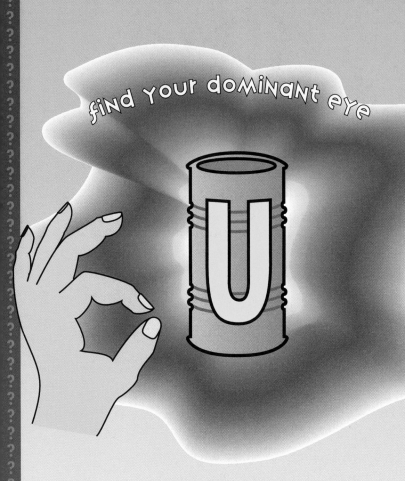

Mirror Message:

The world is out there and is real. But how you perceive or understand it is inside you and is stuff you make by yourself, for yourself.

wrong answer to this test!

P.S. from Beakman: Some of you will have your right eye dominant and others will have the left eye dominant. Just like right- or left-handedness, both are fine. Both work. There is no

48

Dear Jax,

Why are down feathers warm?

Sam Zehr
Mount Pleasant,
Pennsylvania

Dear Sam,

Everything in the universe is trying to be the same temperature. Cold things warm up and hot things cool off, and this keeps on happening until everything is the same temperature. Sometimes this is uncomfortable.

What you call cold is really just the lack of heat. Heat is a kind of energy and cold is what happens when there is less heat energy.

Down feathers slow the movement of heat from you to the cold outside. The heat you feel is really your own body heat, made by you from the food you ate.

Jax Place
Jax Place

49

A Class Act

WHAT YOU NEED: Classroom microscope - feather - poly-puff (a synthetic cottonball used for first aid or makeup) - school encyclopedia

WHAT TO DO: Look up feathers, artificial fibers and thermodynamics in the encyclopedia. There will be pictures to look at. Set up the microscope and look at the feather. Compare it to a bit of the poly-puff. Let classmates look at both, as well.

poly fibers

SO WHAT: That little fluff ball is made out of the same stuff we use to fill jackets and sleeping bags. It's not as expensive as feathers; it does not look at all like feathers, but does have lots of places for air to get trapped. This makes it a good insulator and a good thing to keep warm with.

Feathers

All the little air pockets in feathers and the poly-puff slow down the movement of heat. When air is caught in separate little pockets that stay still, the movement of heat is slowed down.

P.S. from Beakman: Real down feathers are still a better insulator than artificial fibers like polyester. We still can't make fibers that are as lightweight and that trap air as well as down.

51

Dear Timothy,

At certain times of year, like Halloween, I get a lot of questions about weird stuff like ghosts and dreams. The only answer I can give you is that *You Can* read while you're dreaming if you're dreaming that you're reading.

See, dreams and dreaming are not things that happen to us. Dreams are something we make up for ourselves. No one can tell you what you can or cannot dream. It's up to you. Really.

Beakman
Beakman Place

Playing With Words

WHAT YOU NEED: Pencil - paper - active imagination - help from your family

WHAT TO DO: Go into any room of your home. Divide the paper into 2 columns. Ask someone to pick out any object in the room. Write down its name in the first column.

In the second column, write down all the things it reminds you of. This is where you need your imagination and help. *You Can* come up with at least 10 things any 1 thing reminds you of. Do all this for 5 items. It'll be a fun thing to do together.

SO WHAT: You just acted out the difference between your conscious (KAHN-shus) and unconscious (un-KAHN-shus) minds. Our conscious mind keeps track of very literal stuff, like a thing's name. Your unconscious is a bit more playful and isn't limited by things like time and space. It can list very wild and unexpected things.

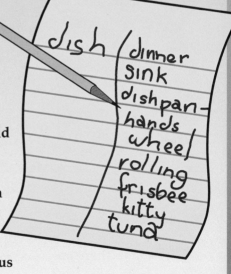

dish | dinner
sink
dishpan-hands
wheel
rolling
frisbee
kitty
tuna

When you go to sleep, your conscious mind is shut down for the night. That leaves the unconscious mind free to party. That's what your dreams are – your unconscious mind going over your list in a free-form, playful kind of way.

53

EXPERIMENT #2

Direct Your Dreams

WHAT YOU NEED: Just your sweet self.

WHAT TO DO: Pick a color that you'd like to see in a dream. As you fall asleep, think of all the things that color reminds you of. Keep adding to the list of things your color reminds you of until you fall asleep.

SO WHAT: If you keep doing this, night after night, you will eventually see your color in your dream. You'll also know that it's there because you wanted it to be there. And it will feel great!

P.S. from Jax: Directing your own dreams takes time. Be patient with yourself. And keep working at it.

Dear Luke,

That sounds like a shivering-beside-the-swimming-pool, where's-the-towel, teeth-chattering question. It sends a chill up my spine just to think about it. (You might get one in a couple of seconds.)

The water on your skin needs heat energy to dry. That energy is going to come from you, from your body heat.

You feel colder because heat moves from you to the water on your skin, which makes it possible for the water to turn into a gas and float away. When it does float away, it takes that heat along for the ride.

Jax Place
Jax Place

Turning a Liquid into Gases

WHAT YOU NEED: A grown-up - rubbing alcohol - tissue

WHAT TO DO: ⚠️Rubbing alcohol can be very dangerous stuff, so get a grown-up to help. Grown-ups like to think they are teaching you something. They enjoy that and will lend a hand. Ask for help working with the alcohol.

Rub an alcohol-soaked tissue onto the back of your hand.

Gently blow. Watch the wet spots as you blow, and feel the temperature of your hand.

SO WHAT: Your hand felt like ice, and *evaporation* is the reason why. Evaporation is when a liquid turns into a gas. That's what happens when something dries. Cold alcohol will not evaporate (ee-VAP-or-ate). The heat it needed came from your hand. As the alcohol drifted away, it took the heat from your hand with it. Water does the same thing, only slower. Both make you cold.

Hospitals used to use alcohol to cool down people with fevers. It was rubbed on patients' skin, which is why it's called *rubbing* alcohol.

P.S. from Beakman: The reason you see those wavy lines on the bottom of the pool is that water bends light. The sunlight is bent and unbent as waves and ripples float by on the top of the water. An artist named David Hockney likes to make pictures of them.

Turning a Gas into Liquid

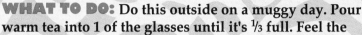

WHAT YOU NEED: Warm tea - 2 glasses - ice

WHAT TO DO: Do this outside on a muggy day. Pour warm tea into 1 of the glasses until it's $\frac{1}{3}$ full. Feel the outside of the glass. Next, fill the glass with enough ice to make iced tea. When it's really cold, look at the outside of the glass.

Use the second glass to make a nice glass of iced tea for a friend.

SO WHAT: This is the opposite of Experiment #1. The warm glass was dry. When you added ice, the cold glass absorbed heat from the air. This chilled the air next to the glass, and cold air cannot hold very much water vapor, a gas. The water vapor had to turn back into a liquid, which formed all those wet drips on the outside of the glass.

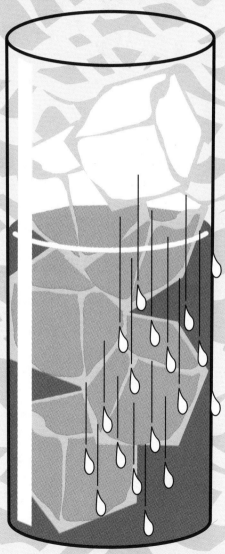

Dear Beakman,

Why don't coniferous trees lose their needles in the winter?

Damien Dery
École Secondaire Le Caron
Penetanguishene, Ontario

Dear Damien,

Now that's a really big word – *coniferous*. So it looks like already you know a lot. You know that coniferous (ko-NIF-ur-us) trees are the ones that have their seeds in cones and usually have needles.

Here's a news flash for you: Some conifers do lose their needles in the fall. Trees like the Dawn Redwood turn color and drop needles every autumn.

But I think you're asking about most pines and evergreens. The reason they stay green is their chemical factories don't need that much power to make food. If that doesn't make sense, read on.

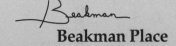

Beakman Place

Leaf Collecting

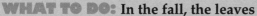

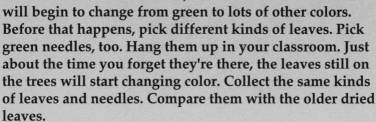
EXPERIMENT #1

WHAT YOU NEED: An active imagination - patience - autumn

WHAT TO DO: In the fall, the leaves will begin to change from green to lots of other colors. Before that happens, pick different kinds of leaves. Pick green needles, too. Hang them up in your classroom. Just about the time you forget they're there, the leaves still on the trees will start changing color. Collect the same kinds of leaves and needles. Compare them with the older dried leaves.

SO WHAT: Lots of people think that leaves change color when they dry out. But that's not true. The leaves and needles you picked first are still green even though they are very dry.

Imagine your leaves are chemical factories. They all use sunlight as their power. What they do is make glucose, a kind of sugar. It's food. When the factory is on, the leaves are green. When the factory shuts down, the color green is pulled out of the leaf, and the other colors can then be seen.

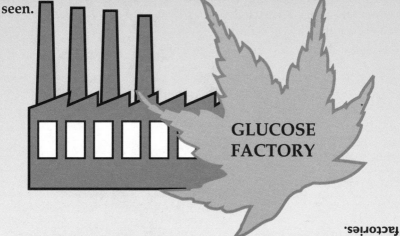

GLUCOSE FACTORY

P.S. from Jax: When leaves change color, they've really only lost the color green. The other colors were there all along. The green is from chlorophyll – a chemical plants use in their chemical factories.

59

Needles Are Leaves

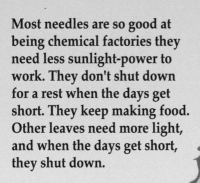

Damien's entire class at École Secondaire Le Caron wrote me letters on recycled paper they made themselves! Thanks for saving those trees.

Most needles are so good at being chemical factories they need less sunlight-power to work. They don't shut down for a rest when the days get short. They keep making food. Other leaves need more light, and when the days get short, they shut down.

Dear Jax,

What are fingernails made of?

**Brandon Gramse
Murray, Utah**

Dear Brandon,

This is going to sound weird, OK? Nails are made out of the same thing as steering wheels – sort of. In the 1930s Henry Ford started making plastic steering wheels out of the protein in soybeans. In a way, your body does the very same thing.

Nails are made from the protein keratin – and the building blocks for it have to come from plants. By the way, nails are made out of the same stuff as horse hooves, bird talons and feathers, bull horns, bear claws and hair.

Jax Place

Keratin

All proteins are very complicated molecules. They're big and strong, and our bodies use them like building blocks. Proteins are a part of just about everything in our bodies.

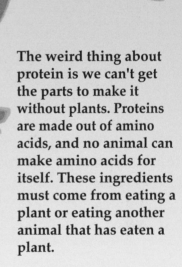

The weird thing about protein is we can't get the parts to make it without plants. Proteins are made out of amino acids, and no animal can make amino acids for itself. These ingredients must come from eating a plant or eating another animal that has eaten a plant.

P.S. from Beakman: It takes about 6 months for your fingernails to grow from the root all the way out to the nail tip. Your toenails take 2 to 3 times as long.

62

Fingernail Facts

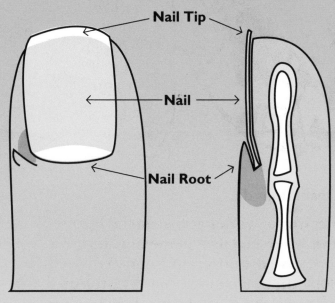

Nail Tip

Nail

Nail Root

Your nails grow a lot like hair. They grow from a nail root that is under the end of your nails. This is the only part of your nails that is alive. The part that shows is dead. That's why it doesn't hurt to cut them. But when you get a hangnail, you've accidentally opened up the edge of the living nail root. And, YOW – it hurts!

The next time you trim your nails, examine the clippings closely. If you have a microscope at school, *You Can* see the protein fibers. Try to pull a clipping apart. The proteins are so strong you'll probably have to twist and *tear* it in two.

Dear Amanda,

Fireworks work because metal burns, and when metals and metal-salts burn, they give off different colors. We usually don't think of something like iron as burning. But it can burn – bright white.

Fireworks use intense heat to burn metals and metal-salts. The heat comes from gunpowder, which is mostly fine granules of charcoal with other chemicals added.

Experiments with fire are *not* a good idea because they are extremely dangerous. But there is an experiment your family can do to show you that metals can burn. ⚠Do not try this without help from a grown-up! Okay? Okay.

Beakman
Beakman

Burning Metals

EXPERIMENT #1

WHAT YOU NEED: Magnet - permission and help from a grown-up - the glowing, burning coals left over from a cookout - safety goggles

WHAT TO DO: Put on your safety glasses to protect your eyes. Drag the magnet around in the gutters of a paved street. ⚠ Be very careful. Do not do this if cars are zooming around. Safety is the first reason why you need a grown-up to help. Save the fuzzy black stuff that sticks to the magnet until you have ¼ to ½ teaspoon. Wash your hands well.

MORE STUFF:
When it's dark, ask your grown-up helper to sprinkle the black powder onto the glowing coals. Pay close attention. There will be a very short, bright white sparkle. ⚠ *Note: The powder you burned is not good to handle. It's another grown-up-type thing.*

WHAT IS GOING ON: The sparkle comes from burning steel. A sparkler works something like this, only with a fuel that keeps burning the steel for a longer time.

SO WHAT: All fireworks work the same way – a metal or metal-salt for color and a fuel that gets incredibly hot to burn it up. The black powder you got from the street is rather upsetting. It's really *powdered car parts*. As cars drive, they give off little shavings of metal. If you weren't able to find very much of it, you're lucky. It means your street is free of this kind of pollution.

65

Days to Celebrate

July 1
The day Canada celebrates the nation's birthday.

July 4
The day the U.S.A. celebrates the nation's birthday.

After your family cooks the mystery-meat hot dogs on the grill, the glowing coals can demonstrate metals burning.

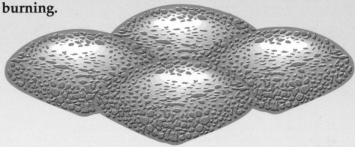

P.S. from Jax: Salt that we eat is only 1 kind of salt. Salts are made when acids react with metals – or things that behave like metals. Sodium chloride, table salt, is made from chlorine and the metal sodium.

Dear Jax,

How do fish breathe under water? I'm in the 7th grade and still don't know.

Jennifer Hastings
San Antonio, Texas

Dear Jennifer,

Don't feel bad about not understanding something regardless of what age you are. The key thing is asking when you don't. And that's exactly what you did. Lots and lots of people don't know the truth about fish.

Fish do not breathe under water. Breathing is the way we get oxygen into our blood and get waste gases out. Fish use a different method.

Jax Place

Oxygen in Water

WHAT YOU NEED: Just a glass of water

WHAT TO DO: Leave the glass on a table beside your bed. Go to sleep. In the morning, you'll see little bubbles in the glass. Those tiny bubbles are filled with air that was dissolved in the water. That's what fish use for their oxygen. Water flows over the gills, which are full of tiny blood vessels.

Letting Gases In

WHAT YOU NEED: Balloon - patience

WHAT TO DO: Blow up the balloon and tie it off. Now just let it sit somewhere. In 2 days you'll see that it has deflated.

WHAT IS GOING ON: The air inside passed right through the rubber! It's called osmosis (oz-MO-sis). Gases dissolved in water go through fish's blood vessels the same way.

Take a Closer Look

The next time you're at a grocery store that sells fish, conduct an examination. Open up the gills and have a look-see inside. (You can't hurt the fish anymore. It's already laid out on a bed of cracked ice.) Inside the gills you'll see the red, oxygen-absorbing tissue. If you slide a pencil inside the gills, *You Can* unfold them and look more closely.

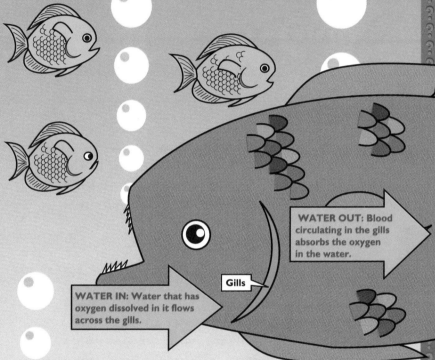

WATER OUT: Blood circulating in the gills absorbs the oxygen in the water.

WATER IN: Water that has oxygen dissolved in it flows across the gills.

Gills

Mirror Message:
The reason for bubbles in an aquarium is not just to look pretty. They're there to put oxygen into the water for the fish to use.

Sharks swim with their mouths open to force water over their gills.

P.S. from Beakman: The next time you see a shark swimming on TV, look at its mouth. It's always open.

69

Dear Beakman,

What does the reduction of our ozone have to do with global warming?

Timothy Hood
Lake Forest, California

Dear Timothy,

The only things I can think of are that both were created by humans and both have been explained very badly by the press. So badly, lots of people write me to ask what trees and ozone have to do with each other.

So let's set it all straight right here, OK?

The ozone layer and global warming are 2 *separate things*. They are caused by 2 separate things humans do to the planet. *They are not related.* Each one is a very big problem.

We can't solve either one of them until we can all understand what's going on.

Beakman

Beakman Place

Global Warming: Heat

Problem #1 - The Greenhouse Effect

WHAT YOU NEED: 2 empty jars - water

WHAT TO DO: Put a teaspoon of water in each jar. Put the lid on just 1 jar. Lay both in a sunny spot. In several hours, take a look at the jars. The open jar will be pretty much the same. The closed jar will be steamy and hot inside. The heat from the sun could not escape.

SO WHAT: When we burn oil, coal or wood, we release carbon dioxide (CO_2) gas into the air.

CO_2 slows down the movement of heat – it insulates. More CO_2 in our air is like putting the planet inside a tremendous closed jar. Earth gets more and more heat from the sun, but it can't cool off. It gets warmer.

When we plant trees, we create a place to store the carbon in CO_2. Trees take the carbon out of the air and put it into storage. This is 1 reason why the rainforests are so important – they're places the planet can store carbon.

Ozone Layer: Light

Sunglasses for the Planet

Earth is bathed in light and other energy from the sun all the time. Not all of that energy is healthy. One kind of energy that's not good is called ultraviolet radiation – usually we say UV or UV-rays for short.

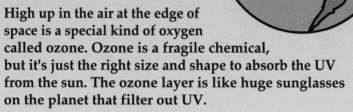

High up in the air at the edge of space is a special kind of oxygen called ozone. Ozone is a fragile chemical, but it's just the right size and shape to absorb the UV from the sun. The ozone layer is like huge sunglasses on the planet that filter out UV.

But the ozone seems to be being destroyed by chemicals called CFCs. They are used in refrigerators, and lots were used in spray cans. Spray cans in the U.S.A. no longer use CFCs.

The next time you hear someone mention ozone in the same sentence with trees and the greenhouse effect, politely explain that they're separate things. Tell them all about planets with sunglasses and planets in closed jars.

Mirror Message:
The third big problem is acid rain. And guess what? It's yet another separate problem that has nothing to do with the other 2. Acid rain happens when rain falls from the clouds and goes through clouds of polluted air containing sulfur from coal or oil fires. That turns the rain into weak acid, which can kill plants and lakes.

Dear Beakman,

What makes the pupil of your eye turn red when you get your picture taken?

Lorraine Dufour
Headingley, Manitoba

Dear Lorraine,

Great question! The thing that makes cats' eyes seem to glow and the thing that makes the fenders of a bicycle seem to light up is the exact same thing that makes your eyes seem to glow in some flash pictures.

It's light that's bouncing. Think of light as a basketball. It gets thrown into your eyeballs by the flash. The light bounces around inside your eyes. And if your eyes are open far enough, some of that light will bounce back out into the camera.

It can make you look all weird, which is perfect for times like autumn and Halloween when people actually like to look weird.

Beakman
Beakman Place

EXPERIMENT #1

Getting the
Red Out

WHAT YOU NEED: 2 flash cameras - 2 photographers - a group of friends who can get into the idea of looking weird

WHAT TO DO: Wait until evening, when light is low. Don't turn on all the lights – just enough to see. Set up a pose with the people in the room. *Make sure they're all looking directly toward the cameras.* The cameras should be right beside each other. One of the photographers should start counting. Both photographers should get ready to take a picture.

MORE STUFF: On 3, take the first picture. Take the second on 5. Tell your friends that it's going to happen this way so they can keep their pose.

SO WHAT: The first picture should have some red eyes in it. That's because people's eyes will open wide to let them see well in the dimly lit room. The light from the first camera will make people's eyes close down, so there will be fewer red eyes in the picture taken with the second camera.

Deep into Your Eyes

When there isn't much light, the iris (EYE-ris) in our eyes opens up around the pupil. That lets in more light.

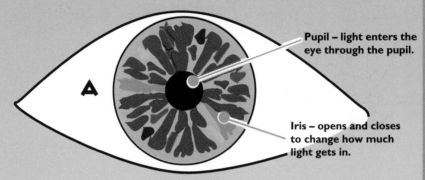

Pupil – light enters the eye through the pupil.

Iris – opens and closes to change how much light gets in.

Eye A is what your eye looks like in bright sunlight.

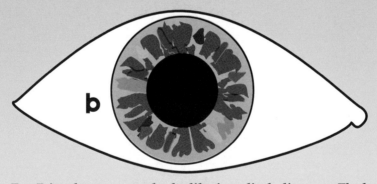

Eye B is what your eye looks like in a dimly lit room. Flash photos shine a really bright light into your eyes. The light bounces around inside your eyes. If your iris is open, some of the light will bounce back out into the camera. The light that bounces back out is what makes you look weird.

Try this: Sit in a dark room – like the bathroom – for several minutes. Turn on the light and look into a mirror. Look closely into your eyes. *You Can* actually see the iris close the pupil.

P.S. from Jax: Something else that seems to glow is really only bounced light. It's the moon, which bounces light from the sun.

Dear Jax,

What is hail made out of?

Libby Henriksen
Salt Lake City, Utah

Dear Libby,

Hailstones are Nature's jawbreakers! They're little bits of ice built up layer by layer as they get blown up and down inside huge clouds. Most of the time, hail is the size of a BB pellet.

But in some cases hailstones get to be as big as a golf ball or bigger. When that happens, falling hail can break windows. This is why people kind of go nuts when hail starts falling. They cover up and run for shelter. There's a special kind of concern we all have about being caught in the hail. Maybe golf ball-sized hailstones are in the back of our minds.

Jax Place

EXPERIMENT #1

Hail Happens

WHAT YOU NEED: Pancakes for breakfast (I wish!) - an active imagination

WHAT TO DO: The next time someone makes pancakes (or any other batter or dough), just stick your finger in. When you pull it out, you'll get a layer of batter. If you were to let it dry and stick your finger in again, you'd pick up another layer. Eventually, you'd have a ball of batter as big as a golf ball! That should remind you of things like hailstones.

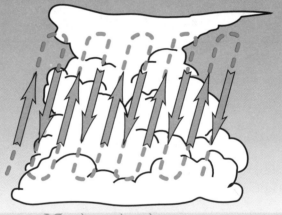

SO WHAT: Hail begins as a tiny droplet of water that gets caught in a powerful wind. It gets blown up into a tall, frigid cloud.

As the droplet blows upward, it freezes. Then it falls and picks up a new layer of water. But the wind keeps blowing it back up into the freezing cold, where the water freezes into a new layer of ice.

This will keep happening until the layers build up so thick the wind can no longer lift the hailstone up into the sky. That's when it falls on us below.

77

Jawbreakers & Hailstones

Jawbreakers have brighter colors than hailstones and are sweeter. But they're built pretty much the same way – layer by layer.

A jawbreaker is hard, jaw- (and teeth-) breaking candy built up in layers of sugar. *You Can* see the layers as the sugar dissolves.

A hailstone is a frozen droplet of water surrounded by layers and layers of ice.

The more trips up inside the cloud, the more layers and the bigger the hailstone gets.

P.S. from Beakman: Snow is different from hail. Snow is a frozen crystal that grows into a beautiful 6-pointed flake. Hail is pretty much just a lump of ice.

Dear Beakman,

How do you make ink?

Darcy Azzopardi
Toronto, Canada

Dear Darcy,

There's lots going on with ink. It is not just a dye in water. The colored stuff in ink does not dissolve in the liquid part of ink. The color just sort of floats in the liquid – suspended.

The color is called the pigment. The liquid is called the vehicle. And there's another part – the binder, which sticks the pigment onto the paper.

By the way, printing inks are different from writing inks. Printing inks are a lot like paint and are made with oil. It's a kind of pollution. Many printers are switching over to soy-based inks, which do not pollute.

Beakman
Beakman Place

EXPERIMENT #1

Thousand-Year Ink

WHAT YOU NEED: Charcoal - foil - hammer - honey - water - fine-point brush

WHAT TO DO: Place the charcoal in between 2 pieces of foil. With the hammer, smash, crack and crunch it up. Keep pounding until you have a *very fine* powder. (If you don't have any charcoal, ask a grown-up to scrape about 2 tablespoons of soot from the inside of a fireplace.) For every 2 tablespoons of charcoal, mix in 2 teaspoons honey. Make a thick black paste. Smoosh it out into a flat square.

MORE STUFF: *You Can* use the ink immediately if you like. But if you let the flat square sit in the sun for several days, it will dry into a solid cake of ink. The finer your powdered charcoal, the better your ink will be.

Use your ink by wetting your brush and stroking it against the ink.

The pigment is the carbon in your charcoal or soot. The vehicle is the water, and the binder is the honey.

Ink made this way has lasted for thousands of years. It was invented in the Middle East by ancient Arabs.

P.S. from Jax: The ink that most cartoonists use is made a lot like your ink – with carbon as the pigment. It's called *India ink* and it too lasts a very long time.

The planet Jupiter was hit on July 19, 1994 by lots of enormous comet chunks.

A comet named Shoemaker-Levy-9 broke up in 1993. Then it looked like *pearls on a necklace*. Big pearls! On a gigantic necklace! Aimed right for Jupiter!

The comet chunks were 1½ to 3 miles across. And there were more than 20 of them, zooming along at 133,920 miles an hour. That's more than 37 miles a second!

Beakman & Jax Place

380 Years Ago

Famous Dead Guy in Science

Galileo Galilei   (1564-1642)

In 1610, Galileo made himself a telescope and looked at the planet Jupiter.

He saw that Jupiter had its own moons! He drew this picture of the 4 moons he could see circling Jupiter.

With photos from space probes, we know that Jupiter has a dust ring like Saturn does. And lots of moons – 16 of them!

P.S. from Beakman: Read more about Jupiter at your library. Books on Jupiter usually have the number 523.45.

Jupiter Is Gigantic

Jupiter is way huge! Its diameter is as big as 11 of Earth's diameters. If Jupiter were hollow, you could put 1,300 Earths inside of it.

All of the dots and swirls on Jupiter are probably enormous storms. The largest is called the Great Red Spot. It's bigger than 2 whole planet Earths!

The comet chunks made tremendous explosions on Jupiter. But we were safe here on Earth. Jupiter is farther away from Earth than the sun is. So these explosions could not hurt us.

Dear Jax,

When you turn off the light, where does the electricity go?

Ashley Taranta
Largo, Florida

Dear Jax,

Why does the light in the refrigerator go on and off when I open or close the door?

Emily Gehlhausen
Ferdinand, Indiana

Dear Jax,

Why do we need the dark?

Ashley Soares
Redwood City, California

Dear Ashley, Emily and Ashley,

I liked how your questions kind of flowed into each other.

The answers to all three have to do with things flowing.

So let's go with the flow.

Jax Place
Jax Place

Flowing Electrons

Electricity is not a thing. Instead, it's when something happens. It's when electrons flow through a loop.

When you turn off a light, you break the loop and stop the electrons from carrying energy through the circuit. The electricity does not go someplace else.

It's just not happening anymore.

Breaking the Flow

Look inside the edge of your refrigerator doorway. You'll find a button of some kind right where the door will push it when you close the door. That's a switch. The switch breaks the loop and stops the electrons from flowing through the circuit. That means electricity isn't happening anymore, and the light bulb goes out.

Mirror Message: What's wrong with the drawing of the light bulb?

The switch is open. The loop is broken. The bulb can NOT light up without the loop.

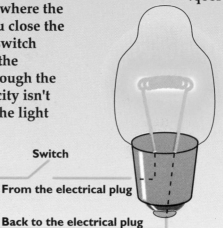

Switch

From the electrical plug

Back to the electrical plug

Energy Flowing

I don't know if we *need* to have dark. That's what Ashley asked about. Things do not exist just because we need them to. And darkness isn't even a thing anyway.

Instead, darkness is what there is when light is missing. Light is energy. Darkness is when light energy has been blocked.

You cannot make dark. No device can ever be made that can make dark. If you want darkness, the only way to get it is to keep out light or block the light. Sounds a little like a poem, doesn't it?

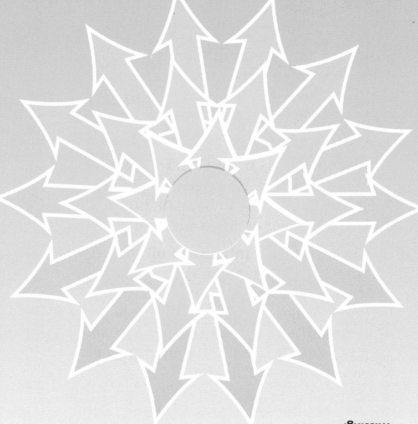

P.S. from Beakman: The refrigerator in Emily's question does not make cold. Instead, it removes heat. Cold is a lot like dark. Cold isn't a thing, either. Cold is the absence of heat. It's when heat is missing.

Dear Jax,

How is mayonnaise made?

Mary-Frances
Bartels
Denver, Colorado

Dear Mary-Frances,

People love their mayonnaise so much they seem to put it on everything – even corned beef.

Mayonnaise is truly a miracle of the material world. It's something that shouldn't be able to happen, but does! Oil and water *do* mix in mayonnaise!

Mayo is a thick mixture of oil and vinegar. (Vinegar is mostly water.) But try to mix those 2 things together, and they always separate. Yet right there on your halftime-show sandwich they do mix! We call that kind of mixture an emulsion (ee-MUL-shun).

Jax Place

The Mayo Clinic

WHAT YOU NEED: 2 egg yolks - 1 teaspoon salt - 1 tablespoon vinegar - 1 cup vegetable (or olive) oil - family help or permission - blender *Optional: lecithin powder (from health food store)*

WHAT TO DO: Take the center out of the blender lid. Put the egg yolks into the blender with the salt and vinegar and whip until it's light and fluffy. Add the oil *drop by drop* while the yolks are still being beaten. This takes *a lot* of time. Do not be in a hurry or the oil globs will touch each other and the mayonnaise will turn into mayo-soup. When the mayo gets thick, stop adding oil.

SO WHAT: If your eggs aren't fresh, you'll end up with mayo-soup. If that starts to happen, immediately add a pinch of lecithin powder. That will turn the mayo-soup back into mayonnaise.

If your mayo doesn't get thick, try again with fresh eggs and with more patience, adding the oil much slower. Or add less oil.

Mayonnaise takes practice. But then again, you are making something that shouldn't even exist, and that can be difficult.

ITZA MIRACLE
MAYONNAISE

Math Skills Are Valuable

WHAT YOU NEED: 50 pennies or other coins - a friend
Optional: 50 pebbles, 50 sticks

WHAT TO DO: Ask your friend to play a little game with you. Explain that you both can take turns removing up to four pennies from the pile of coins. The person who has the last turn wins. You will always be able to win and the reason is knowledge of math.

Part of the trick is convincing your friend to take the first turn. After that, it's subtraction and division.

MORE STUFF TO DO: Remember the number 5. Make sure that your coins plus the number your friend takes always add up to be 5. If your pal takes 4, you take 1.

If you continue to subtract the number of coins your friend takes from the number 5, and use the answer as the number of coins you take, you'll always get to take the last turn – and win.

SO WHAT: This works because 5 divides evenly into 50, and the most pennies *You Can* take at once is only 4. So *You Can* control how many turns there are.

The problem with this kind of thing as a bet to make money is it's a trick – *rigged*. Which means it's like stealing. You can't trick people out of their money and be a whole, happy, healthy person. At least that's what I think. You decide. How do you feel about it?

A Closer Look at Quarters

75% copper
25% nickel

100% copper

75% copper
25% nickel

You Can see 3 layers on a quarter. The shiny, silvery-looking top and bottom are there just for looks – to look like real silver. Quarters made before 1964 were made out of silver – a valuable metal. Even though today's quarters look like silver, there is *no silver or gold at all* in any U.S. coin that is used for money.

P.S. from Jax: The copper/nickel sandwich that U.S. coins are made from is created with explosions! An explosive is spread on the outside of the nickel layers. When it goes off, it bonds them to the copper center.

Dear Christina,

Scientists need a bit of glamour to get the money it takes to research stuff. And *mosquito spit* just isn't that glamorous, even though that's why you itch.

Mosquitoes inject you with it. One of the chemicals in the spit is called apyrase (ay-PIE-raze). *Pyr* means fire, as in: burning itch you just have to scratch.

We don't know much about the other things in mosquito spit because there are only a few people on the planet looking into this burning question.

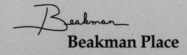
Beakman Place

EXPERIMENT #1

Sacrifice Yourself for Science

WHAT YOU NEED: Serendipity - a warm evening - mosquitoes - healthy dislike for the little bloodsuckers

WHAT TO DO: Let's face it. The next time you're sitting outside in the evening, you may just find a mosquito on your skin, sucking up blood. If you do, pay close attention; conduct an examination. Watch what she does. If you look closely, *You Can* see a little tube sticking into your arm. It's like a hollow tongue.

Now stop and think a minute, here. Isn't blood too thick to travel through that teeny, tiny tube?

WHAT IS GOING ON: Blood has these little cork-like things floating in it called *platelets*. Whenever there's a leak, platelets rush in to start plugging it and stop the flow of blood.

That kind of kevorks the idea of blood sucking. But mosquitoes come prepared. The chemicals they inject into you – like apyrase – shut off the platelets and allow the blood to flow freely. Unfortunately, the spit they're in makes you itch like mad once she flies away.

P.S. from Jax: Mosquito food is really flower nectar. Only female mosquitoes suck blood because they need its protein to lay eggs and make the next generation of these beasties.

95

Up Close & Personal

This is a close-up of a mosquito's eye. Each little dome is a separate lens. It can't see details. But this kind of eye can spot any kind of motion really well.

This is a mosquito's tongue. It's called a proboscis (pro-BOSS-cus). This is what the bug sticks into your skin. Apyrase gets pumped in to keep the blood flowing. On the other end of this thing, the mosquito has actual pumps it uses to suck out your blood.

Electron micrographs: Wilfred Bentham.
Consulting mosquito enthusiast: Glenn Corey.

Dear Misun,

Every time you move a part of your body, you're using 2 muscles to do it. The first muscle moves it. The second muscle moves it back.

People who have big buffed bodybuilder bods do not have more muscles than you. They have just worked to stretch the same muscles we all have.

You Can build a model of an arm joint that will give you an inside view.

Beakman

Beakman Place

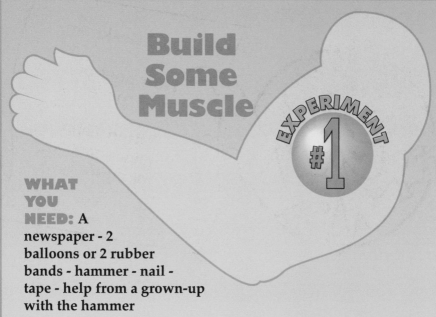

Build Some Muscle

EXPERIMENT #1

WHAT YOU NEED: A newspaper - 2 balloons or 2 rubber bands - hammer - nail - tape - help from a grown-up with the hammer

WHAT TO DO: Open up the paper and roll up 1 full page. Make a tight tube and hold it with tape. Do this 3 times to get 3 tubes. Stack them on top of each other and have your grown-up helper drive a nail through all 3 at 1 end. Bend the middle tube out. Tape together the 2 outside tubes at the other end. Attach the balloons or rubber bands like in the drawing. This is a model of your arm, forearm and elbow!

SO WHAT: If you bend your *arm* back and forth by pulling on the muscle balloons, *You Can* see that they work only in the pull direction. Muscles cannot push. That means you always need 2 muscles, in pairs, to do any and all back-and-forth moving.

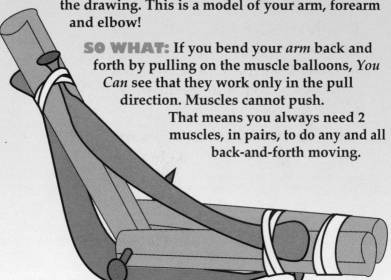

Getting All Uptight

Muscles are made of muscle cells, and muscle cells do only 1 thing – get uptight. Your muscles work by getting shorter. We call that *contracting*. All muscles work in only 1 direction. Muscles do *NOT* push out. They *ONLY* pull in.

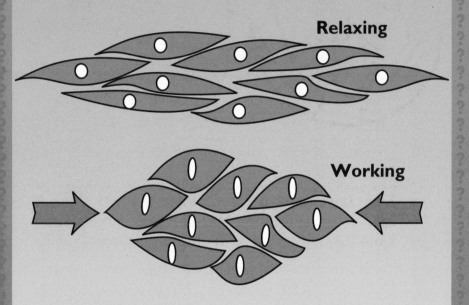

Relaxing

Working

SO WHAT: When you bend your elbow to lift your arm, the muscle on top of your arm pulls in. When you lower your arm, that muscle doesn't do anything at all – it relaxes. What lowers your arm is the muscle on the back of your arm pulling in.

Mirror Message:
Muscle on top of arm: bicep.
Muscle on back of arm: tricep.

P.S. from Jax: Your muscles will never turn to fat, even though some people say so – usually out-of-shape people. Muscle and fat are 2 separate things. Muscle cells are muscle cells and will always be muscle cells. Ditto for fat cells.

Dear Jax,

How do you make napkins pretty?

Sara Wooden
Baltimore,
Maryland

Dear Sara,

To make a napkin *You Can* use any soft and absorbent paper. *You Can* also make a napkin with a piece of cloth.

To make a napkin *pretty*, you have to use more – a lot more. You have to use *geometry*.

Every once in a while, some sexist bozo will say that girls don't do well at geometry – the math of shapes. Well, I don't think that's true.

I think any girl (or boy) who can turn a limp Scotties into a dazzling dish-top display has geometry mastered – and has a real flair for entertaining as well.

Jax Place
Jax Place

The Crowning Touch

WHAT YOU NEED: Paper or cloth napkin - a little patience

WHAT TO DO: Follow this procedure. When you get it, fold several and stand them up on plates for dinner tonight.

1

Start with a square. A square has 4 sides that are all the same length and 4 corners that are 90 degrees each. If you're using a paper napkin, start by opening it up to give you a big square to work with.

2

Fold the square in half. That gives you a rectangle – 4 90-degree corners and sides that are not all the same.

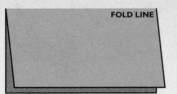

FOLD LINE

3

Fold the top corner down and the opposing corner up. That makes a parallelogram, which is the shape in drawing #4. It's like a rectangle relaxing and leaning over.

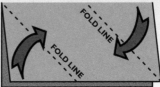

FOLD LINE
FOLD LINE

4

Turn the whole thing over and fold it in half along the dotted line. Let the peak of the triangle flip up so that it looks like drawing #5.

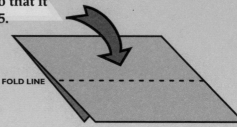

FOLD LINE

5

So now your napkin looks a little like 2 pyramids connected with a bridge. Fold in each side on the 2 dotted lines.

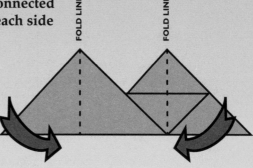

FOLD LINE   FOLD LINE

6

Tuck the end of the pyramid inside the flap you'll find on the other pyramid. Now, just stand it up and open the inside so that it looks like a crown.

This standing napkin has lots of shapes and is also a terrific way to impress visiting relatives. Make as many as *You Can*.

TUCK

P.S. from Beakman: When you fold flat paper into the shapes of other things, you're doing the art of origami. There are books on origami (and on many different napkin folds) at your library. Borrow them for free!

Dear Edgar,

When you see radical stuff in an ornament, you're not really looking *into* the ornament.

You're seeing bounced light – light bouncing off stuff in the room that bounces off the curved glass ball.

After the gifts are open and the wrapping paper has been wadded up, take a few minutes to look at the room by collecting light with a glass tree ornament.

Jax Place

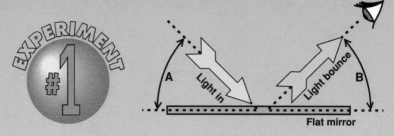

A   Light in   Light bounce   B

Flat mirror

Bounce Some Light Around

WHAT YOU NEED: Mirror - shiny ornament

WHAT TO DO: Take some time to see what *You Can* see in a mirror. Everything you see is light bouncing off the mirror into your eyes. Angle A will always equal angle B. That's why you can't see stuff that's directly beside the mirror. You can't get close enough to the wall to make the angles equal. Try it.

MORE STUFF: Look at the ornament. Light coming in from wide-apart things and places will be bounced into your eye. Things that are beside the ball will be reflected into your eye. The ornament is a sphere, and its surface faces *all* directions.

That's what's special. Because the surface of the ornament is curved, it can face your eye and something beside the ornament at the same time.

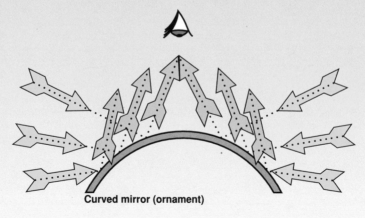

Curved mirror (ornament)

Ornament
Reflections

P.S. from Beakman: Take an ornament off the tree and put it up where you do your homework. Leave it there all year. *You Can* use it to see most of the room behind you, just by glancing up. It's also good for a daydream.

Dear Jax,

How do you make macaroni?

Craig Linton
Dublin, Ohio

Dear Craig,

Long ago, before there were shopping channels on cable TV selling us fake jewelry and pasta machines, we used to call it macaroni – or even noodles. Now it seems as though everyone uses the word "pasta."

Maybe the word pasta is better because it's so close to another word that explains what noodles are really all about – *paste*. Pasta and paste have very similar recipes.

Most pasta is made by extrusion (x-TRU-shun), which means it is squirted out of special nozzles that give it special shapes – just like you can see on a shopping channel.

Jax Place
Jax Place

Make Pasta

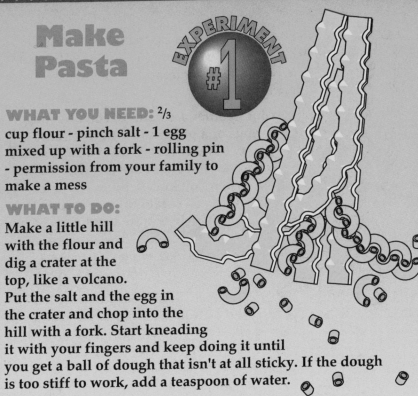

EXPERIMENT #1

WHAT YOU NEED: $2/3$ cup flour - pinch salt - 1 egg mixed up with a fork - rolling pin - permission from your family to make a mess

WHAT TO DO: Make a little hill with the flour and dig a crater at the top, like a volcano. Put the salt and the egg in the crater and chop into the hill with a fork. Start kneading it with your fingers and keep doing it until you get a ball of dough that isn't at all sticky. If the dough is too stiff to work, add a teaspoon of water.

MORE STUFF: Let the ball sit for $1/2$ hour. Spread some flour on a cutting board. Roll out the ball on top of the flour until you get a thin layer of dough. Use a butter knife to cut the thin dough into long strips. If you want, trim them to any length you like. Cover with a towel until they dry.

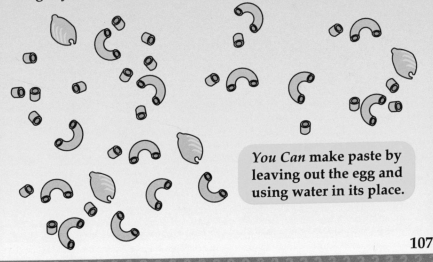

You Can make paste by leaving out the egg and using water in its place.

107

SO WHAT: Ask a grown-up to boil your dried noodles. *You Can* serve them in soup or with a bit of melted butter or margarine. They'll be delicious!

Your noodles are held together by long strings of a protein in wheat called *gluten* (GLOO-ten). Gluten absorbs a lot of water, but is not dissolved in water. When you knead gluten, it's a lot like you're tangling up fishing line into a big, knotted and very strong mess. These tangled strings are what gives wheat paste its strength, too.

The eggs in your noodles provided color, fat and water. Machine-made pasta doesn't need eggs at all and can easily be made with water – or vegetable juices, which is where all that colored pasta comes from.

PASTA WORDS:

Noodle - From the German word "nudel"

Spaghetti - Italian for "little strings"

Linguine - Italian for "little tongues"

Vermicelli - Italian for "little worms"

Macaroni - 18th-century British slang for someone who tries to impress you with his or her knowledge of Europe. Not a compliment.

P.S. from Beakman: Gluten is something you eat every day. The walls of all those thousands of tiny bubbles in bread are made from kneaded gluten.

Dear Jax,

What is black pepper made of? Where does it come from?

Terry Dobyns
Streator, Illinois

Dear Terry,

Here's a little bet you can win with someone today. Black peppercorns come from: a. pepper trees; b. peppers; c. corn; d. vines or e. shrubs?

When the early European explorers were out looking for a sailing route to the East, they were trying to find an easier way to get black pepper from Indonesia.

The bet is hard because we use the word *pepper* to describe lots of things – from cayenne or trees to jalapeño.

The correct answer is vines, up to 12 feet tall! They still grow in the spice islands of South East Asia.

Jax Place
Jax Place

109

Pepper Power

WHAT YOU NEED: Black pepper - bar of soap - toothpick - bowl of water

WHAT TO DO: Let the water get very, very still and quiet. Shake black pepper onto the water until the whole surface is covered with floating pepper.

Just touch the water with the toothpick. Be very gentle and still. Try not to disturb the pepper with the toothpick. Do the same thing with the corner of a bar of soap. Just touch it and pull it back. Compare what happened with the toothpick to what happened with the soap.

SO WHAT: OK, you got me. This has very little to do with what black pepper is made out of. It's just a fun thing to do with pepper.

The pepper sits on top of a kind of skin the water has, called the surface tension. The toothpick doesn't bother it. But the soap breaks that skin and the pepper jumps back as the skin breaks and jumps back.

The pepper jumps back from the soap in a split second!

110

photo: Chloe Atkins

A microscope shows us that black pepper isn't really black. The berries are picked from the vine when they're green and then allowed to sit in the sun for a while. A black fungus called *Glomerella cingulata* grows on the skins. Yum! That's the only part that's black, the fungus. Green pepper is made by skipping the fungus-growing part. White pepper starts off as green pepper, but then the green skin is rubbed off.

P.S. from Beakman: The chemical in black pepper that makes us sneeze is called piperine (PIE-pur-een). It irritates our nose, and a sneeze is a kind of convulsion we have to clean it out.

Dear Beakman,

Where do potholes come from?

Rodney Piña
Sausalito, California

Dear Rodney,

Potholes happen. And when the snow melts in most places, you're going to see (and feel) pavement pits.

Asphalt (AZ-fawlt) is the stuff lots of roads are made from. But asphalt is a lot like a sponge – porous and not solid. That's one reason these road eruptions occur.

When roads fill with potholes, people get all angry. But what are you going to do? Go complain to city hall? Maybe. And with today's experiments, *You Can* know what you're talking about when you do.

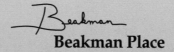

Beakman Place

Absorbing the Shock of It All

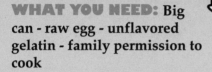

WHAT YOU NEED: Big can - raw egg - unflavored gelatin - family permission to cook

WHAT TO DO: Make up a batch of gelatin that is 4 times as strong as the directions tell you. (Use 4 times the gelatin.) Pour it in the big can till it's about ⅓ full. Chill till firm.

Place the egg on top of the jelled junk and completely fill the can with more gelatin. *Make sure the egg does not touch the can.* Chill till firm.

Now drop the can outside. Keep dropping it from higher and higher places until the egg breaks. *Note:* The bigger the can, the better this works. With a big No. 10 can, *You Can* drop it from as high as a roof and the egg inside will not break.

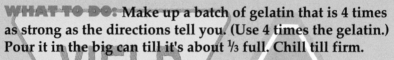

WHAT IS GOING ON: When the can hits the ground, energy from the impact is transferred to the can and then to the gelatin. The gelatin spreads that energy out because it's springy. The springs and shock absorbers in your car work the same way. You and the car are isolated from the shock of hitting street-zits.

P.S. from Jax: Rodney's last name has an interesting letter in it: ñ. You say its name like this: EN-nyah. It's used a lot in Spanish. We do not say PEE-na. We say PEE-nyah.

113

Alligators?

All potholes begin with *base failure*. Asphalt is made of gravel, sand and thick tar. That's the base, or bottom layer in a road.

It's covered with a fine tar – the road surface. Pressure moves the road base, and little cracks appear on the road surface called alligator cracks.

Once the alligator cracks are formed, water will flow into the road base. As cars drive over it, the water sloshes

back and forth in the crack, pulling apart the asphalt. Or the water can freeze. Both will pop open a pothole.

Fill a pop bottle all the way with water – to the very top. Stick it in the freezer till it's solid. Notice the water got bigger. When that happens inside a road, the surface pops off and makes a pothole.

Dear Ricky,

The answer is kind of surprising. It's all wrapped up in how we name stuff. Even though cold has a name, cold is not really a thing.

We only have more heat or less heat. When we say that something is cold, what is really going on is there is less heat.

That means that refrigerators do not make cold. You can't make something that is not a thing in the first place. What a refrigerator really does is *move heat*.

Jax Place
Jax Place

Getting Cool

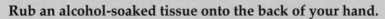

WHAT YOU NEED: A grown-up - rubbing alcohol - tissue

WHAT TO DO:

⚠ Rubbing alcohol can be dangerous stuff, so get a grown-up to help. Do this together with your family.

Rub an alcohol-soaked tissue onto the back of your hand.

Gently blow. Watch the wet spots as you blow, and feel the temperature of your hand. (You may have done this experiment earlier when we looked at why you get cold at a pool.)

SO WHAT: You got really cold, and *evaporation* is the reason why. Evaporation is when a liquid turns into a gas. Cold alcohol will not evaporate (ee-VAP-or-ate). The heat it needed moved from your hand.

Inside your refrigerator is a loop of pipes filled with a chemical that can do the same thing – change from a liquid to a gas and move heat as it evaporates.

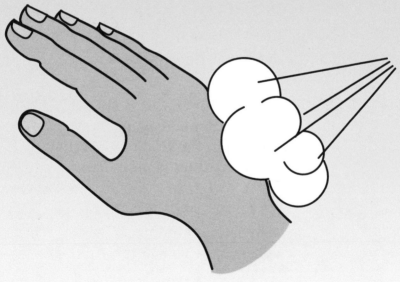

116

Moving Heat Around

1 The liquid chemical is inside these pipes. Heat moves from your food to the liquid, which evaporates and turns into a gas.

3 The liquid goes to a coil outside the refrigerator, where the heat moves again. This time the heat moves from the coils to the air in your kitchen.

Evaporator Coil

1

3
Condenser Coil

2
Compressor

Find the coils outside your fridge. Feel them. They'll be warm. That's the moved heat that used to be in your food.

2 The gas goes into a compressor, which squeezes it back down in size until it becomes a liquid again. But the heat in the gas has to go somewhere. It can't just disappear, because nothing ever disappears!

P.S. from Beakman: The chemical inside your refrigerator that evaporates and moves heat is called Freon™. We didn't know about it for a long time, but we now know that it can cause a very serious kind of pollution.

Dear Beakman,

Can you please tell me how to make rock candy?

**Roger Relucio
Elizabeth,
New Jersey**

Dear Roger,

Rock candy is a great way to see what crystals are about. Rock candy is just crystallized sugar.

⚠️You absolutely need a grown-up to help you with this experiment because it involves cooking sugars at dangerous temperatures hot enough to burn or hurt you badly.

Beakman
Beakman Place

ROCK OUT!

WHAT YOU NEED: 2 cups water - 5 cups sugar - pie pan - string or bamboo skewer - grown-up - candy thermometer - foil - patience

WHAT TO DO: Stretch the string across a pie pan so that it is suspended across the top. You'll have to weight the ends so that it does not touch the bottom of the pan. Or *You Can* punch holes in the edge of the pan and tie the string. *You Can* also lay a skewer across and out the pan like in the drawing.

MORE STUFF: Dissolve the sugar in the water and cook until it reaches 250°. This temperature is also called *hard ball*, and most cookbooks will tell you how to do it without a candy thermometer. Don't stir after you've dissolved the sugar.

P.S. from Jax: There was so much sugar dissolved, the water couldn't hold it all. Some sugar had to undissolve and grew into sugar crystals.

119

EVEN MORE STUFF: Pour the hot liquid into the pan. The string should be ³/₄ inch under the surface of the sugar water. Cover the pan with foil and *don't touch it for a whole week*. In 7 days, lift out the string or stick and it will be covered with sugar crystals!

Dear Beakman,

How are rubber bands made?

Michael Craig
Freehold,
New Jersey

Dear Michael,

Rubber bands are one of those things that are all over the place, even though we don't think about them much. So first, congratulations for thinking freely.

Rubber bands are made by extrusion (x-TRU-shun), which is a fancy way of saying they're squirted out of a special machine.

You Can use another method, a warm summer day and some weeds to make your own rubber band!

Beakman
Beakman Place

Make Your Own Rubber Band

EXPERIMENT #1

WHAT YOU NEED: Dandelions or milkweeds

WHAT TO DO: Break the leaves and roots of the plants until a white milky sap oozes out. Coat your first finger with this and let it dry in the sun. Add more layers of sap, letting each one dry. Gently roll the dried sap down off your finger.

SO WHAT: The sap in the plants is a lot like latex, the tree sap from which rubber is made. If you stretch your little rubber band gently, you'll feel its stretchiness – we call that *tensile cohesion* (TEN-sul co-HE-shun).

Rubber is stretchy because it's made out of molecules shaped like long springy strings. When you pull out and then let go, the molecules pull back into their original shape.

Your rubber band is not very strong, because we cheated on getting real latex and used weeds instead of rubber trees.

Lots of Loops

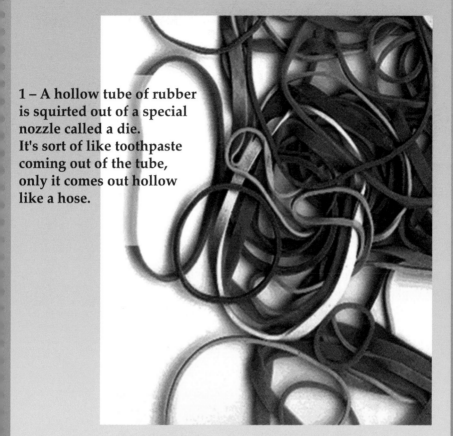

1 – A hollow tube of rubber is squirted out of a special nozzle called a die. It's sort of like toothpaste coming out of the tube, only it comes out hollow like a hose.

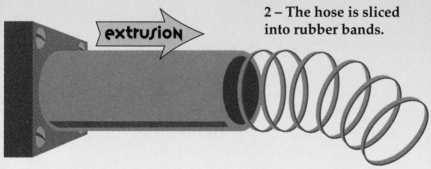

extrusion

2 – The hose is sliced into rubber bands.

P.S. from Jax: Every year rubber band factories make about 85,000,000 rubber bands. The best customer for them is the U.S. Postal Service, which puts $8^1/_2$ billion bands around mail every year.

123

Dear Jax,

Where does the salt in ocean water come from?

Kristin Flower
Potterville,
Michigan

Dear Kristin,

Water flowing over and through land keeps bringing minerals to the ocean. Then the water goes back to the land – as rain, leaving the minerals behind in the seawater, where they keep getting stronger.

We say the minerals in seawater get *concentrated* (CON-sen-tray-ted) by the never-ending cycle of evaporation.

By the way, it's not just salt that ends up in the oceans. There are dozens of minerals in seawater. Salt is just the one with the greatest concentration.

Jax Place
Jax Place

The Evaporation Cycle

6 It starts all over again with the rain flowing into the land.

5 The water vapor condenses into clouds that return to land and make rain.

1 Water runs down and through the land, collecting in ponds, lakes and rivers that drain to the oceans.

4 Water evaporates into water vapor, leaving the salt behind. More and more salt keeps getting left behind.

2 On this long, long trip the water picks up and dissolves lots of minerals, including salt.

3 The water arrives at the ocean as very weak saltwater.

What's a Concentrate?

WHAT YOU NEED: Frozen orange juice

WHAT TO DO: Let the o.j. melt until it's a thick liquid. Reach in with your finger and then take a lick. Finish by following the directions on the can and make the orange juice.

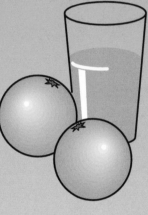

SO WHAT: What you tasted was orange juice with most of the water taken out. That made it extra-strong o.j. We call that a *concentrate*. Seawater is mineral water with most of the water removed. That concentrates minerals like salt.

Make a Concentrate

WHAT YOU NEED: Salt - water - measuring cup - plate - patience

WHAT TO DO: Add ¼ cup salt to 1 cup hot water. Stir until it dissolves. Pour some of your saltwater into a pie plate that you've set near a heater vent. Now ignore it for several days. Check on it until the water is dried.

WHAT IS GOING ON: The water part of the saltwater evaporated (ee-VAP-or-a-ted). The water turned into water vapor and went into the air. The salt was left behind. That's why ocean water gets salty – the water keeps evaporating and leaving behind the minerals it brought to the sea.

P.S. from Beakman: Besides salt, ocean water also includes dissolved calcium, potassium, magnesium, sulfur, zinc, copper, iodine, iron, phosphorus, manganese and more!

Dear Beakman,

Does the spin of the Earth change the seasons?

**Julia Burnett
Olathe, Kansas**

Dear Julia,

Earth spins a lot like a top while it travels in a big circle around the sun. This huge top – Earth – tilts over in its spin, and this *tilt of the spin* is what changes our seasons.

Most college graduates taking a general knowledge test think that the seasons change because of the Earth's distance from the sun. That's wrong.

Find yourself a college graduate. Explain the whole thing – the Earth's tilt is why we have seasons.

Beakman

Beakman Place

127

Pretend You're the Sun

WHAT YOU NEED: Flashlight - darkness

WHAT TO DO: Turn off the lights. Hold the flashlight about 2 feet from a wall and turn it on. Now raise your arm until you're shining the light on the wall, up near the ceiling.

Look for differences in the way the light shines with your arm lowered and raised.

SO WHAT: When the light was shining directly at the wall, it was strong with lots of energy. When you raised your arm, the light spread out and so did the energy.

Summer is when the solar energy is direct and strong. Winter is when the solar energy is spread out. Spring and fall are in-between times.

Unlike your flashlight, the sun does not change its angle.

Winter Sunlight

Summer Sunlight

P.S. from Jax: If the Earth was not tilted, the amount of solar energy you got wouldn't change from day to day. That means there wouldn't be any change in the seasons at all. (Unless you count the beginning of the baseball season.)

What Season is It?

Look at the orbit of the Earth and notice which hemisphere is pointing toward the sun. Hold the page up to a mirror to read the answers.

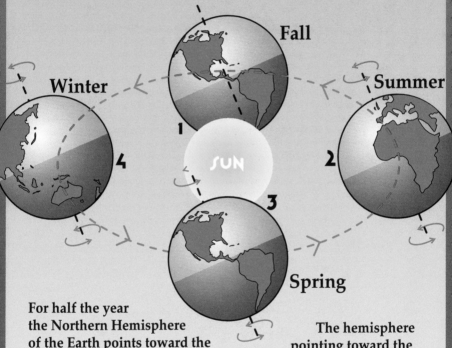

Fall

Winter

Summer

SUN

Spring

For half the year the Northern Hemisphere of the Earth points toward the sun.

For the other half-year, the southern part of the planet points toward the sun.

The hemisphere pointing toward the sun is having summer. The other hemisphere is having winter. Springtime happens when the axis starts pointing back toward the sun. Fall happens when it starts pointing away.

Dear Jax,

Why are bubbles round and not cubes?

Laura Sutherland
Concord, California

Dear Jax,

Why do cats curl up into a ball?

Kara Vesely
Walnut Creek, California

Dear Kara and Laura,

Cats and bubbles are round like balls for the same reason. They're working to be small.

The shape that does that better than any other is a ball – a sphere (sfeer). Cats try to be as small as possible to stay warm. The smaller they are, the less skin is exposed to the cold outside air.

Bubbles do it because soap film always shrinks to be as small as it can be. The smallest shape bubbles can be and still contain the same amount of air as a ball. These experiments are better to do than read about!

Jax Place
Jax Place

Shrinking Soap Film

WHAT YOU NEED: 2 cups dishwashing soap - water - rubber band

WHAT TO DO: Add the soap to a sink of water and stir well. Get your hands all wet and soapy. Stretch the rubber band over your fingers, turning and twisting it into weird shapes. Dip it into the soapy water and then lift it out.

SO WHAT: You got some pretty strange-looking soap films. That's because the film shrinks to its smallest possible shape.

Try it with a friend's helping hands. The shapes can get even stranger with 2 people.

P.S. from Beakman: Think about the reason cats stretch out in the summer. If curling up into a ball keeps them warm, what does stretching out do?

131

Getting Extreme

WHAT YOU NEED: Coat hangers - sink of soapy water from Experiment #1

WHAT TO DO: Bend the coat hangers into twisted springs and tangled messes of wire. Just make sure that the tangles do not touch each other when the wires cross. Take the time to pull touching places apart.

MORE STUFF: Hold the hook and dip the whole thing into the sink. Pull it out slowly. The soap film will look like a beautiful twisted slide.

Try other shapes. Just make sure the wires do not touch when they cross.

Mirror Message:

Now that you've got a sink full of soapy water, help out and do the dishes!

Dear Beakman,

If you traveled as fast as the sun, how fast would you go?

Laura Hathorn
Spokane,
Washington

Dear Laura,

There's no *if* about it. You already are traveling as fast as the sun. That's because where the sun goes, the Earth goes with it.

The sun is on a long, strange trip orbiting the center of our galaxy, the Milky Way.

The trip takes 250 million years (for 1 orbit) and is really fast – 480,000 miles per hour. But that's just 1 of the speeds we're traveling.

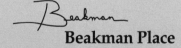
Beakman Place

Everything's Always Moving
It's all Relative

Your speed depends on what you are comparing your speed against. Your speed relative to the floor is 0 miles per hour when you're standing still. But since you're on the Earth, you have other speeds: your speed relative to the axis of the Earth, your speed relative to the center of the sun, and your speed relative to the center of our galaxy, the Milky Way.

Here's a way to imagine the route we take through the universe: Imagine you're climbing a spiral staircase, while you're spinning around and around. That's just about what's happening to all of us on Earth right now!

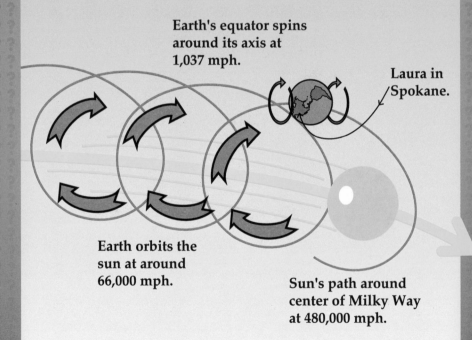

Earth's equator spins around its axis at 1,037 mph.

Laura in Spokane.

Earth orbits the sun at around 66,000 mph.

Sun's path around center of Milky Way at 480,000 mph.

Light-Years Away

This is the galaxy named M31. Astronomers think the galaxy we're inside of looks a lot like M31. Our galaxy, the Milky Way, is 80,000 light-years wide. A light-year is *NOT* a measure of time. Instead, it's a distance: how far light would travel through a vacuum in 1 Earth year. One light-year is 5,878,000,000,000 miles. 80,000 light-years is 470,240,000,000,000,000 miles.

M31 is in the constellation Andromeda (an-DROM-e-da) and is about 2,200,000 light-years from Earth.

P.S. from Jax: There are about 100,000,000,000 stars in the Milky Way. Now get ready for this: There are billions of galaxies! And they too are all moving all the time!

Dear Scott,

Your TV's remote control works by sending out a beam of invisible radiation that's a lot like light. It's called infrared radiation (IN-fra-red).

You Can see how this stuff works by bouncing this energy around the room or down the halls.

If you live with channel-surfers, and you're tired of the channels getting changed every second, *You Can* use your knowledge to wipe them out.

Beakman

Beakman Place

Bouncing the Beams

WHAT YOU NEED: Remote control - TV - mirrors *Optional: Shiny cooking pot lid - flashlight*

WHAT TO DO: Point the remote away from the TV and try turning it on. Now use the mirrors to set up a twisted, all-bent-up path. If you can see a reflection of the TV in any number of mirrors, you can use the remote control. Even if you're in another room!

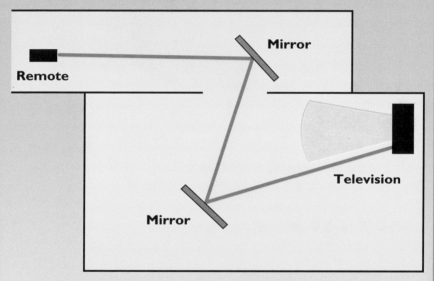

Remote

Mirror

Mirror

Television

MORE STUFF: If you don't have mirrors to use, aim your remote into the inside of a cooking pot lid. *You Can* use the lid as a reflector and aim the infrared beams all over the place.

Use a flashlight to closely examine the end of your remote control. Notice the color of the little window on the end.

P.S. from Jax: There are 2 ways to wipe out channel surfers. Hide the remote, or put a piece of black tape on the little window on the remote. Trim it neatly so that it won't be noticed. It will block the beams.

Light and the Universe

This is going to sound cosmic because it is!

Light is a set of waves. Other waves are radio waves, X-rays and infrared energy. If you arrange the waves by their size, you get something called the *electromagnetic spectrum*. Visible light is just a very small part of it. Infrared radiation has longer waves than light.

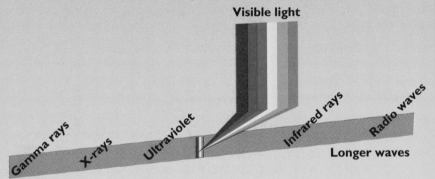

Visible light

Gamma rays   X-rays   Ultraviolet   Infrared rays   Radio waves

Shorter waves   **Longer waves**

Most light bulbs make infrared rays in addition to the light rays we think of first. We can filter out the visible light, which will turn the bulb into an infrared beam machine.

WHAT IS GOING ON: Your remote sends out coded pulses of infrared beams. They bounce off mirrors and shiny surfaces just like light, only we can't see them. Each button on the remote control sends out its own code of flashes. The TV is programmed to do certain things when a receiver cell picks up the beams.

Behind the window are little light makers called **LEDs**. The window is a filter that removes their visible light but lets the infrared radiation shine through. The **LEDs** pulse with a code every time you push a button.

138

Dear Beakman,

Down at the mall there are lots of people with their eyes crossed, looking at 3-D posters. How do they work?

Robert Goldstone
Bloomington, Indiana

Dear Robert,

We recognize things like form, color and distance.

In the 1960s a psychologist named Bela Julesz made 3-D pictures with random dots – visual noise – to see if people could perceive distance without any clues from form or color. His 3-D dot pictures work because humans get used to patterns: repetitive, regular, predictable, repetitive. The pictures give us a regular pattern that is upset slightly.

Our minds move the upset pattern forward or backward to make it seem like it fits into the pattern again. That's what reveals the hidden images. It also feels very trippy and spacey.

Beakman

Beakman Place

139

Seeing Things

WHAT YOU NEED: Just your sweet self

WHAT TO DO: Look at the flies on the wall. Notice the 4 dots above the flies. Cross your eyes *slightly*, until you see 5 dots. Let your attention drift back down to the flies. They'll be floating!

Next, put the page right up to your nose. Focus your eyes as though you were looking across the room. Slowly take the page away from your face. If you start focusing on the page, *start over again*. Eventually, you'll see the flies float again. Only this time the little flies will be closest to you and the big ones will be farthest away. The distances will be reversed.

WHAT IS GOING ON: Both methods work because each of your eyes sees its own separate part of the fly pattern. Each part of the fly pattern is different, so your brain works to put them together by adding the sense of depth. The second method is called *averted view* and is how most of the 3-D posters work. If you cross your eyes at the posters, you'll reverse the distances and lose the hidden image. You'll see holes where you should be seeing things like whales or dolphins. Practice *averted view* on this simple version before your next trip to the mall. *And give yourself time!*

P.S. from Jax: Sometimes when we get spaced out (meditative), we can seem to see depth in things like carpeting, tree bark, sidewalk sparkles, acoustical ceiling tile or certain wallpapers. It's the same effect without a trip to the mall.

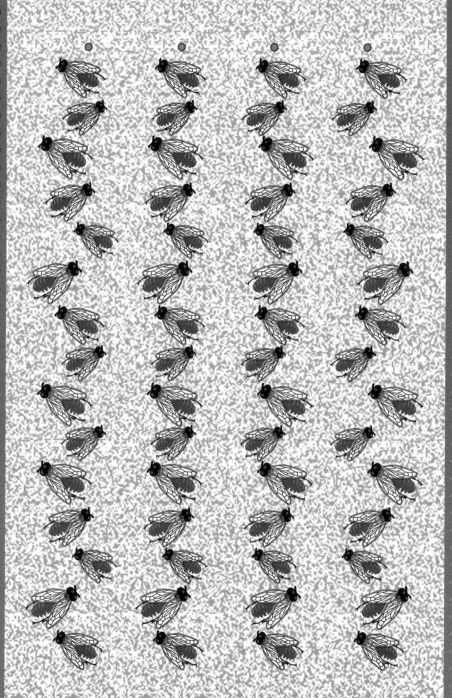

141

Dear Amy Marie,

Thunder is not made out of a thing. Thunder is a thing that happens. If we could see thunder, it would probably look like the design behind the next page – sound waves pushed and pushing through the air.

Thunder is a huge, enormous push of sound waves. The push is from the heat of a tremendous electrical spark – the lightning. Thunder is the sound we hear from an explosion.

The air around the lightning gets very, very hot and expands really quickly. And that's what an explosion really is – when something gets really big, really quickly.

Jax Place

Jax Place

EXPERIMENT #1

Poppa's Got a Brand-New Bag!

WHAT YOU NEED: Paper bag

WHAT TO DO: Hold the bag to your mouth and blow it up. When the bag is full of air, close the end. I'll bet you already know what's next: Pop the bag!

Maybe you've done this before but never thought about thunder before. So think about thunder for a minute.

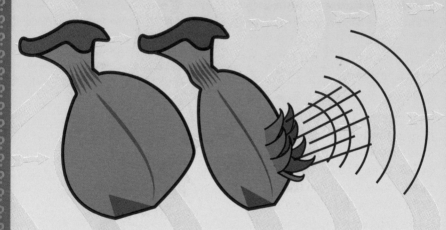

SO WHAT: When you popped the bag, you gave the air inside a big squeeze. It rushed out the hole, pushing against the air outside the bag.

It was kind of a shoving match. The air in the bag pushed against the air outside, which kept pushing air and pushing air until these shock waves got to your eardrum – which turned them into hearable sounds. That's a lot like thunder, only thunder is a lot bigger.

P.S. from Beakman: Thunder can tell you how far away lightning is. When you see the flash of light, start counting slowly. Stop counting when you hear the thunder. Divide the number of seconds you counted by 5. That's the distance in miles.

143

Expanding Air

WHAT YOU NEED: Balloon - glass soda bottle - saucepan - water - stove - help and permission from a grown-up

WHAT TO DO: Stretch the mouth of the balloon over the mouth of the bottle. Place the bottle in the saucepan and slowly pour steaming hot water around the bottle – about 2 inches. (Ask a grown-up to boil the water and to pour it.) Sit back and watch what happens to the balloon.

WHAT IS GOING ON: The heat energy you put into the air inside the bottle made the molecules of air move more quickly, and to do that, they need more room. So the air just expands and takes up more room. That's why the balloon filled up with air.

Thunder is air getting real hot from a lightning bolt, and expanding so quickly that it explodes.

144

Dear Beakman,

Are tree rings made from the inside or the outside of the tree?

Nate Witkin
Akron, Ohio

Dear Nate,

Yes, tree rings *are* made from the inside or the outside. I hope that's not too confusing. The rings form inside the bark and outside the old wood.

Rings form as trees enclose last year's growth in a new living envelope. This happens every year underneath the bark, which is a dead, protective layer.

When it's spring, the trees are shifting into high gear – growth-wise, I mean. You know, putting out leaves and growing a new ring of wood.

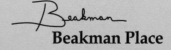
Beakman Place

EXPERIMENT #1

A Closer Look

WHAT YOU NEED: The perfect moment

WHAT TO DO: The perfect moment for this examination is the next time you see a broken tree branch. You might choose to break one yourself, or you might choose to wait until the next time you see one. Either way will work and be just what you need.

Carefully peel off the bark. Look inside the bark for a soft living layer. Scratch it with your fingernail. The branch itself will be shiny and very pale. If the break is clean, look at the end of the branch. Look for the rings and notice how they are different. Some are thick. Some are thin. Start with the biggest ring and count inward the same number of years as your age. When you get to the number that's your age, you'll have a better idea of how long trees take to grow.

If you don't have a tree branch handy, *You Can* do the same count with a piece of lumber.

Wouldn't today be a great day to plant a tree?!

P.S. from Jax: Not all trees make rings. Palm trees are filled with fibers. Banana trees are like huge pieces of celery. They have a few veins and soft, water-filled flesh.

Inside a Tree

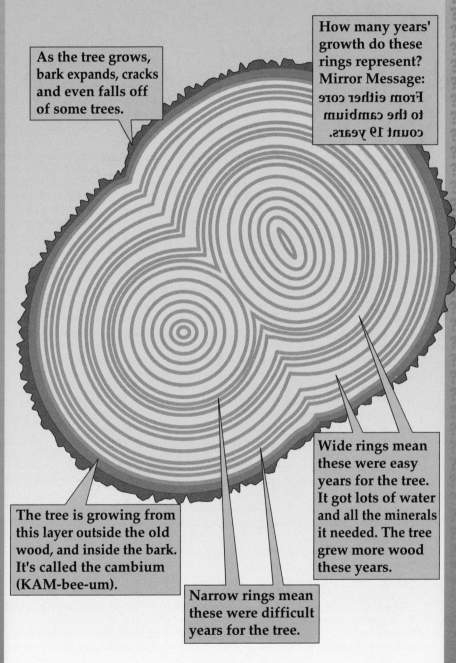

As the tree grows, bark expands, cracks and even falls off of some trees.

How many years' growth do these rings represent? Mirror Message: *From either core to the cambium count 19 years.*

The tree is growing from this layer outside the old wood, and inside the bark. It's called the cambium (KAM-bee-um).

Narrow rings mean these were difficult years for the tree.

Wide rings mean these were easy years for the tree. It got lots of water and all the minerals it needed. The tree grew more wood these years.

147

Dear Beakman,

What is water made out of?

Mark Andrew & Rachel Ann Numan New Hamburg, Ontario

Dear Mark and Rachel,

If you read labels, you'll see that water is the main ingredient in everything from soda to shampoo. So it's interesting to find out that water has its own ingredients, too.

Water is made out of oxygen and hydrogen. Two hydrogen atoms are bonded to 1 oxygen atom. *You Can* write the formula like this: H_2O. (It might make a little more sense if we wrote it like this: H_2O_1.)

Beakman

Beakman Place

Take Water Apart

WHAT YOU NEED: 9-volt battery - bowl - 2 small glass jars - tape - insulated wire - ¼ cup white vinegar - grown-up

WHAT TO DO: Cut the wire into 2 pieces and strip off the insulation from all four ends. Tape 1 wire to a snap on top of the battery. Repeat with the other wire and the other snap. Make sure you get a good contact. Fill the bowl with water and add the vinegar. Put in the jars. Then turn the jars over as in the drawing and make sure there is *no air inside them at all*. Put in the wires like in the drawing – *do NOT let them touch each other*. Look closely.

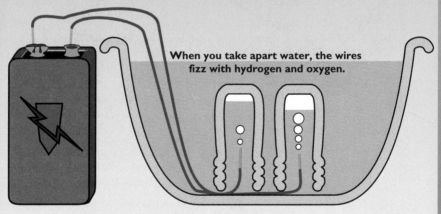

When you take apart water, the wires fizz with hydrogen and oxygen.

⚠ CAUTION: Your experiment uses a low-power battery and is safe. But *NEVER* put any other electrical wires in water. That would be dangerous!

P.S. from Jax: The vinegar helped the water conduct electricity. Taking apart water into hydrogen and oxygen is called electrolysis (ee-lek-TROL-a-sis). Ask your teacher which gas is coming off of which wire and why.

The electrical energy from the battery split the molecules of water apart into their 2 ingredients. The little bubbles you saw in the jars were oxygen gas in one jar and hydrogen gas in the other.

Taking apart water molecules always involves energy, which is the reason we can't get enough hydrogen gas to use as fuel. That's right; your car could be built to run on hydrogen, and hydrogen-powered cars would not pollute.

The big problem we have with this idea is that it takes at least as much energy to separate the hydrogen as we can get back by burning hydrogen. The solution may be to use solar energy to take apart water. *Perhaps it will be you who figures out how, solving the great energy puzzle and giving the world pollution-free power!*

OXYGEN

HYDROGEN

HYDROGEN

Dear Jax,

When I touch the water with my hand, it's warm. But when I put in my foot, it's real hot. Why?

Colin Candy
Cherry Hill, New Jersey

Dear Colin,

There's nothing like a nice warm bath to chill you out. I mean, it relaxes you – even if the temperature of the water can confuse you.

That's exactly what's happening! Your body is sending confusing signals to your brain.

You Can even confuse your brain on purpose. This is a great thing to do with friends and family because other people can watch it and still be really surprised when it's their turn.

Jax Place

Think About It First

Before you do the experiment, think about the steps you go through to fill up the tub, get naked and take a bath.

It goes something like this:

Hand - turns on the tap. It gets warm.

Foot - stands on cold floor. It gets cold.

Hand - feels water as it gets hot. Hand gets warmer.

Foot - still on cold floor. It gets colder.

Your hand gets used to being warm, and your foot gets used to being cold. Your brain gets used to it, too! Bath water will seem cooler to your hand and hot to your foot.

Fooling Your Brain

WHAT YOU NEED: 3 bowls big enough to put your whole hand in - ice water (with ice cubes) - very hot water - room-temperature water

WHAT TO DO: Arrange the bowls like they are in the drawing. Put 1 hand in the ice water and the other in the really hot water. Get used to it. Wait *at least* 2 minutes while your hands get used to the cold and the heat.

Really Hot
Water

Room-Temperature
Water

Ice
Water
with Cubes

MORE STUFF TO DO: After 2 minutes, lift your hands out of the water and put them both in the middle bowl. Close your eyes. Try to tell what temperature the water is. Feel with your left hand. What temperature is the water? Now feel with your right hand. What temperature is the water? It feels both hot and cold at the same time. But how can that be?

P.S. from Beakman: The middle bowl still has warm water in it. Your brain just can't tell anymore. To the hand in the ice water, the middle bowl seems hot. To the other hand, the middle bowl seems cold.

Dear Jax,

When you lick your finger and rub it around the rim of a glass, it makes a sound. Why?

Stacy Ream
Milwaukee, Wisconsin

Dear Stacy,

Thanks for asking. This is a fun one.

Wine glasses singing is what's going on.

You Can even play a song on several glasses lined up to play different notes.

The sounds you hear are like *all* sounds: Stuff vibrating, which vibrates the air, which vibrates your eardrum, which vibrates these teeny bones in your middle ear, which vibrate these even tinier hairlike fibers inside your inner ear, which send sound signals to your brain, which turns all these vibrations into sounds.

Jax Place

Jax Place

Whining Glasses

WHAT YOU NEED: Stemmed glass - water - permission from the owner of the glass ⚠ *CAUTION: Do NOT use a chipped glass! It would cut open your finger and blood is better on the inside!*

WHAT TO DO: Lots of times people put these glasses away for special occasions or holidays. So be sure to ask first.

Put a spoonful of water in the glass. Use one hand to hold down the glass's base. Wet a finger on the other hand and rub it on the edge of the glass. Keep trying different pressures until the glass sings. It will!

WHAT IS GOING ON: Your finger rubbing up against the edge of the glass made the glass vibrate. It's harder to vibrate something bigger. Bigger things vibrate more slowly than little things.

You Can change how much stuff you're vibrating by adding water to the glass. The more water you add, the slower the vibration, and the lower the pitch of the sound.

155

Glass Harmonica

Benjamin Franklin invented a musical instrument called the glass harmonica after futzing around with wineglasses at the dinner table. *You Can* find out what Franklin did with 3 wineglasses and a little water.

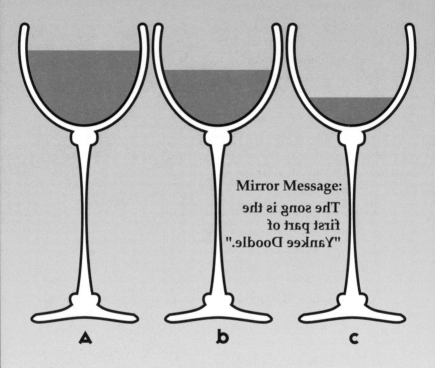

Mirror Message:
The song is the
first part of
"Yankee Doodle".

A   b   c

Play and fill the glasses until you get the notes do, re and mi. Then play this song: A-A-B-C-A-C-B. Franklin asked a glass blower to make different-sized wineglasses without the stem and then nested them together. They spun on a rod. You played by touching the spinning glass.

P.S. from Beakman: Bigger stuff vibrates slower and makes lower-pitched sounds. That's why a tuba has low notes and a little flute or piccolo has high-pitched notes.